Analytical Ayurveda

Dr. K A Latheef

MOTILAL BANARSIDASS PUBLICATIONS

Analytical Ayurveda

First Edition : Delhi, 2019

ISBN : 978-81-940111-0-1

Also available at

MOTILAL BANARSIDASS PUBLICATIONS
41 U.A. Bungalow Road, Jawahar Nagar, Delhi 110 007
1 B, J.S. Compound, Kennedy Bridge, Nana Chowk, Mumbai 400 007
203 Royapettah High Road, Mylapore, Chennai 600 004
49, 8th F Main III Block, Jayanagar, Bengaluru 560 011

MLBD Cataloging-in-Publication Data
Analytical Ayurveda
by Dr. K A Latheef
ISBN : 978-81-940111-0-1
I. Ayurveda II. Pathological Ayurveda III. Etiological Factors
IV. Pharmacodynamics V. Phytochemistry VI. Index

Published by
Motilal Banarsidass Publications
mlbdbooks@gmail.com
Printed by Thomson Press (India) Ltd.

Analytical Ayurveda

Adventure in Consciousness

1

Dedicated to my wife, Zerin and children;

And to my parents and teachers.

Acknowledgement

Many patients expressed the curiosity of how Ayurvedic medicines work. Answer with ambiguous terminologies feel illogical, hence is addressed in the way how I am presenting in this work. Such queries really tempted me to interpret the philosophical principle of Ayurveda, though tough, through the contemporary health sciences. I am thankful to such patients.

I am much obliged to my beloved professor (late) Dr. C. R Agnivesh, a great teacher and writer with immense academic discipline. References from his books also supported me to make this work.

This work was kept aside without publishing. Dr. Murshid, my co-worker happened to find it and forced me to publish it. I am much grateful to him for his technical and moral support.

I also extend my sincere thanks to Dr. Annie. M. Sithara, the female consultant in my clinic, for her diligent proof-reading.

Finally, I expect this work can create a spirit of cooperative interaction among the students who may use it with a view of interpreting Ayurveda. Appreciate them in anticipation.

K. A. Latheef,
"daffdils"
Akkikkavu, Trissur district, Kerala.
drlathif@gmail.com

Ayurvedic Herbal Health Center,
Sharjah, U.A.E
ayurvedicherbalhealthcenter@gmail.com

Contents

PREFACE

Attuned to the principles of Mother Nature, Ayurveda is the 'Science of Health', fully portrayed by philosophy. One who wants to understand this science has no way than understanding those philosophies. Philosophy is the pursuit of wisdom; it is the 'love of wisdom'. The philosophies on which Ayurveda is based are briefed in the following chapters.

Ayurveda waned and perhaps became stagnant in medieval and British Periods. Social stigma attached to blood, dead body or dissection among higher cast members played a major role for this. Its follower's constraints to come out of the conservative philosophies to the updated modern views was another reason. It is important to note that hypothesis and theories are never absolutely proven. A theory is a set of propositions and concepts that provides a reliable, systemic, and rigorous account of an aspect of nature. If a hypothesis continues to survive a testing, it may be accepted as a valid theory.

A science cannot prevail with the "if... and then" reasoning. In a scientific research the hypothesis is falsified and deducted if it is not tested true after the experiments or through the reliable information. If the hypothesis passes the test, it is subjected to more severe testing. The procedure often is made more efficient by constructing and testing alternative hypothesis and refining the hypothesis that survives the testing.

In the modern world Ayurveda had come to the front line. But labels in the contemporary lexicon, such as "mind-body" and "holistic," have connotations of their own and further fail the test of descriptive accuracy.

Ayurvedic students learn their healing 'Science' through the Philosophies, mostly embellished in *Sloga.* In this book I took a strenuous effort to explain Ayurveda using modern scientific terminologies. I regret; it would never have the charm of the real poetic narration of the texts. Hope the students would accept it.

According to Louis Pasteur "Science knows no country, because knowledge belongs to humanity, and is a torch which illuminates the world". Maharshi Charaka emphasized the importance of updating knowledge to practice medicine.

The two ancient manuscripts relevant to the medical developments are *Charaka Samhita* and *Susrutha Samhita* dealing with medicine and surgery respectively.

The descriptions like 'Alternative Medicine,' Integrative medicine,' and 'Complementary medicine' contain the elements that pass the test of compatibility with an expanded view of health. The public's acceptance and use of alternative or complementary medical practices must be interpreted as an indication that these alternative providers fulfill some unmet needs.

It is not wise to search in the fathom of concepts and hypotheses to explain a situation of health crisis. Rather taking unethical initiative to claim the cure of all diseases we treat we should have the humility to express our limitations of old knowledge and expressions. Accept the new methods for explaining facts. That is what the love of science is.

Ayurveda is the way of life. The more we know the more attractive it is. It is against the modernization of the beings surroundings. The negligence of Mother Nature is the main cause of disease. Ayurvedic treatments help body's repairing processes and never cause aggressive destructions as is misinterpreted.

Nithyam hithaahaaravihaara sevi
Sameekshyakaari vishayeshwasaktha:
Daathaa sama: sathyapara:
Kshamavaanaapthovasevi cha
Bhavathyaroa: (AH)

Daily healthy food and exercise, wise activities, avoiding greed, giving capable alms, equianimous, truthfulness, patients, listening to and serving the wise persons are the preventives of diseases!

The content of this book is what I perceived about Ayurveda. The graphs and color code used are my imaginations for the easy method of interpretations. The highlighted columns are the part of an attempt to have a contemporary approach with reference to the classical knowledge as well.

I pledge this book to all those who like to know Ayurveda.

Dr. K. A. Latheef

CHAPTER –1
The Basics of Ayurveda

"Life always accelerates to its end"

It is the definition of 'Life' in Ayurveda.

'Ethi Ithi Ayu' – that which always moves (to its end) is '*Ayu*', the life.

The perfect health is termed as *Swasthya* in Ayurveda.

Ayurveda starts with the advice to those who aspire health (*Ayushkama*)! The chapter is called *Ayushkaameeyam.* To be healthy is difficult unless we follow certain doctrines of the Mother Nature.

The Body–Mind Combination

'D*harma*' is the (Universal) doctrines to be followed in this life. It is the eternal law of cosmos, inherent in the very nature of things. '*Artha*' is the objective goal of this life. '*Sukha*' is the satisfaction or happiness that is gained by *Dharma* and *Artha*. '*Moksha*' is the eternal peace or happiness for which we have to live practicing *Dharma* and gaining *Artha*. The 'material' for conducting *Dharma*, *Artha* and to experience *Sukha* is body (*Darmartha sukha sadhanam Shareera*). Body can perform this only with 'purified conditioned Soul. So when Ayurveda explains perfect health it is applicable to both mind and body.

Vedic view of Ayurveda

Ayurveda is the 'upaveda' (the branch) of *Adharva Veda*. Veda means knowledge. The word came from Sanskrit language and is derived from the root *Vid* 'to know'. Vedas are a sort of manuals showing how to use this world and how to live in it.

Indian philosophy is based on Veda. There are six schools of thoughts in Indian philosophy.

1. *Nyaya*
2. *Vaisheshika*
3. *Samkhya*
4. *Yoga*
5. *Mimamsa*
6. *Vedanta*

1. NYAYA PHILOSOPHY

Goutama wrote *Nyaya sutra* round about fourth or fi fth century it was believed that obtaining valid knowledge was the only way to obtain release from sufferings. Its followers therefore took great pain to identify valid source of knowledge from mere false opinion! According to the *Nyaya School* there are four sources of knowledge

English	Sanskrit
1. PERCEPTION	PRATHYAKSHA
2. INFERENCE	ANUMANA
3. COMPARISON	UPAMANA
4. TESTIMONY	SHABDA

Table 1. Nyaya school of thought

This methodology is well used in Ayurveda and helps even in differential diagnosis of di seases. Nyaya is probably the closest Indian equivalent to contemporary Western analytical philosophy.

The knowledge obtained from various sources is categorized in two types.

1. True Knowledge (Yadhartha njana)
2. Untrue Knowledge (Ayardhartha njana)

True Knowledge (Yadhartha njana)

Perception (*Prathyaksha*)- which for 'Nyaya school of thought' does not deliver mere raw impressions, but is to be recognised as a basic form of cognition, the data of the senses brought into order by mind, and offering us an intelligible view of things as they are. Perception can be determinate, where we perceive the thing as a thing of its kind, a cow as a cow, a shell as a shell, or indeterminate, where we perceive something.

Perceptual knowledge does not come from any more basic form of knowledge; it is based on the contact of the sense organs with their objects. Buddhist philosophers objected to this claim, since in the case of the eyes there seems no contact between the sense organ, for example, a cloud in the sky or a distant hill. The Nyaya answer is that a light -ray from the eye does indeed make contact with the object. Belief in such light rays or eye-rays is not unusual in the ancient world. A present day account would see the 'contact' as made by the light, lamplight, sunlight, reflected from the surface of the thing seen.

Inference (*Anumana*) is a form of knowledge based on existing knowledge. The knowledge on which inference is based can itself come from perception, comparison or testimony. Inference moves from the known to the unknown.

Nyaya sees inference as of three kinds, *cause to effect, effect to cause, and what is commonly seen.* An example for each may make this clear:

- ☐ *Cause to effect*: I see black clouds approaching and infer it is going to rain.
- ☐ *Effect to cause*: I see smoke pouring from the window of my house and infer something is burning.
- ☐ *What is commonly seen*: I see a tall, powerfully built person with a long, full beard and infer the person is male.

It is immediately noticeable that the Nyaya understanding of inference focuses on '*causal relations*' not on what a modern Western philosopher would understand as '*logical relations*'.

Comparison (*Upamana*) again is a form of knowledge based on existing information. The knowledge on which comparison is based can itself come from perception, inference, comparison or testimony. Comparison moves from the known to the unknown.

So far comparison is similar to inference, and critics of Nyaya often argue it is actually a form of inference. Nyaya makes a distinction saying the process is distinct and the way we express it in language is distinct. Unfortunately, modern English use does not support the Nyaya claim. We often express reasoning from comparison by using 'thus' and 'therefore' and 'and so,' the typical marks in ordinary language of inference.

A different distinction can be made: Inference is based on causal relations, comparison on classes (genera, kinds) and their attributes. Unfortunately this still causes problems, since it is not at all obvious why the inference from 'what-is-generally-seen' is not really a mode of reasoning by comparison.

From the point of view of modern logic, the Nyaya account of inference and comparison is inadequate. It fails to uncover the pattern of *logical relations*, which are the ground of the validity of inferences. The Nyaya points to some of the ways in which we reason, and it asserts they are valid, but it fails to show *why* they are valid.

Testimony (*Shabda/Apthopadesham*): The testimony of a relevantly expert person is accepted by Nyaya as a sound source of knowledge.

This certainly corresponds to how we actually come to know and understand things. Indeed, it seems improbable that anyone in history has ever come to knowledge of the world by use of perception, inference and comparison without any reliance on the testimony of others, parents, teachers, friends, associates and so forth. Some viewpoints accept only scriptural statements as testimony. Nyaya, however, distinguishes between knowledge of the visible and knowledge of the invisible, and sees expertise as sufficient to establish the reliability of testimony concerning the visible.

Accepting the four documentations (*pramanas*) as sound means of knowledge does not, for Nyaya, imply that they are infallible. What Nyaya claims about the *pramanas* is that *in general* the four *pramanas* can be trusted and that *as a matter of fact* they are the four sources from which our knowledge is derived.

2. The untrue knowledge or Error (Ayadhartha njana)

Nyaya accepts the existence of error. Most discussion of error in Indian philosophy centers on the possibility, the nature and explanation of *perceptual error*. There is little difficult in accounting for error that arises from use of unsound forms of reasoning or from misuse of sound forms. Perceptual error is more problematic. Does it even make sense to think of the senses as deceiving us? How can I possibly perceive something that is not there? What do I perceive if I do?

The Nyaya account of perceptual error is that error consists in perceiving something as other than it is. Error is always subjective. It arises from three causes:

- ☐ Defect of a sense-organ,
- ☐ Perceiving only a part (and erring because you do not realise what you perceive is only a part of something)
- ☐ Habit or expectation interfering by rousing inappropriate recollections.

Indian philosophers use standard examples to make their positions clear. One standard example of perceptual error is the rope-snake. Nyaya explains the rope-snake as arising from the third cause; I fear to encounter snakes in dark corners and see something like a coil lying in the shadows as a snake.

"*Sasthram saasthrani salilam gunadoshapravrthaye*
pathrapekshinayatha: pragnhyam bahushruthyena brimhayeth"

Weapon, Science and Water show the quality of its container. Beware; intelligence should be nourished with information from multiple sources!

2. VAISHESHIKA PHILOSOPHY

Founded by Sage Kanada, postulates an atomic pluralism that differs from the modern atomic theory. In that the function of atoms was guided or directed by the will of the Supreme Being. Developed independently from Nyaya Sutra, it accepted only Perception (*Prathyaksha*) and Inference (*Anumana*).

Vaisheshika is the teaching of '*Highest good*' -*Dharma*- or Merit which springs elevation (*Moksha*). From this particular kind of merit (*Dharma*) springs true knowledge of certain 'Categories' (*Padartha*). These categories embrace the whole realm of knowledge.

The Categories (*Padartha*) as described by sage Kanada.

1. Matter (*Dravya)*
2. Quality (*Guna)*
3. Action (*Karma)*
4. Genus or Community (*Samanya*)
5. Species or Particularity (*Vishesha*)
6. Inhesion or Inseparability (*Samavaaya*)
7. Negation or Privation, non-existence (*Abhaava*)

These Categories (*Padarthas*) or predicaments were believed to contain an enumeration of all things capable of being named, ie. of being known.

Some disagreed with the *Abhaava* – the non-existence while other philosophers added two more to the Categories (1) Potential (*Shakthi*) and (2) Similitude (*Sadrshya*)

1. The Matter (Dravya)

1.Earth	*Prithwi*
2.Water	*Apah*
3.Light	*Tejah*
4.Air	*Vayu*
5. Ether	*Akaash*

Either eternal or non-eternal and exists in the form of atoms (*anus*) or as material bodies. The impulse given to the atoms comes from God, the *Aatman*, the only one. Others are Innumerable.

6. Time *Kaala*

7. Space *Desha*

8. Self *Aatma*

9. Mind *Mana:*

The principal and characteristic qualities ascribed to Earth (Prithvi) Water (Apah), Light (Tejah) and Air (Vayu) are four, three, two and one respectively

The substance	Characteristic qualities			
Earth	Tangibility	Colour	Taste	Smell
Water	Tangibility	Colour	Taste	
Fire	Tangibility	Colour		
Air	Tangibility			

Table. 2 Qualities of *dravya* (the substances)

But other qualities are mentioned afterwards, making altogether fourteen for earth, such as *colour, taste, smell, touch, number, extension, individuality, conjunction, disjunction, genus, species, gravity, fluidity, and permanence.*

In the case of air, which is invisible, he uses touch as a proof of its existence, also the rustling of leaves; and he does this in order to show that air is not one only. Curiously enough Kanada, after explaining that there is no visible mark of air but that its existence has to be proved by inference and by revelation, takes the opportunity of proving, as it were, by the way, the existence of God

Ether (Aakasha)

Its characteristic quality is sound.

Kanada proceeds to prove the existence of *Aakaasha*, Ether, by showing that it must exist in order to account for the existence of sound, which is a quality, and as such requires the substratum of an eternal and special substance, as shown before.

Time (*Kaala*)

Time, which was one of the eternal substances, is declared to manifest its existence by such marks as priority, posteriority, simultaneity, slowness, and quickness. The arguments in support of the substantiality of air and ether apply to time also, which is one, while its division into past, present, and future, hibernal, vernal, and autumnal, is due to extrinsic circumstances, such as the sun's revolutions. Time itself is one, eternal, and infinite.

Space (*Desha*)

Our perceiving that one thing is remote from or near to another, again, proves Space. Its oneness is proved as in the case of time; and its apparent diversity, such as east, south, west, and north, depends likewise on extrinsic circumstances only, such as the rising and setting of the sun. Like time it is one, eternal, and infinite.

Self (*Aatma*)

The Self must be different from the senses because while the senses apprehend each its own object (*Indriyartha)* only — (1) the sense of hearing, sound; (2) the sense of smelling, odour; (3) the sense of tasting, flavor; (4) the sense of seeing, colour; (5) the sense of feeling, touch — it follows that there must be something else to apprehend them all, the work which in other philosophies was ascribed to *Manas*, at least in the first instance. Besides, the organs of sense (*Indriya)* are but instruments, and as such unconscious, and they require an agent who employs them. If we see a number of chariots skillfully driven, we know there must be a charioteer, and we know also that chariots and horses are different from the charioteer. The same applies to the senses of the body and to the Self, and shows that the senses by themselves could not perform the work that results in cognition.

Mind (*Mana*)

'Manameva jeevitham manushyanambandha mokshay'.

Mind is the cause for both bondage and liberation. It is the 'matter' (*Dravya*) interacting between the senses and intellect (*budhi*). The mechanics of perception (*prathyaksha*), inference (*anumana*), comparison (*upamana*), and memory are due to the involvement of mind. Obviously mind cannot be an object of itself. The chemical and electrical processes in the brain cannot completely explain the mind. This understanding will not account for the faculties of mind including intelligence, consciousness, emotion and volition.

The American Heritage Dictionary of the English Language defines mind as follows: "The collective conscious and unconscious processes in a sentient organism that direct and influence mental and physical behavior." This definition attributes mind to sentient organisms and identifies it with processes that control behavior. According to the view of contemporary science, these are brain and nerve processes, cognition, motor, and sensory processes.

Unfortunately the scientific definition of mind falls short of one important quality, the spirit. Ayurveda being the holistic science is more involved with the spiritual attributes of mind. Satwa, Raja and Tama (See table 4. below) are the qualities of mind. To the Vedic thinker insanity was a condition resulting when the mind leaves the body. The remedy lay in returning the mind to the body. Meditation is the process by which mind is tuned to the physiological needs of the body. Mental and emotional factors are critical to the development of diseases. So the psychosomatic approach is vital in Ayurveda in the diagnosis and treatment.

2. The quality (Guna)

The Matter cannot exist without qualities; as little as qualities can exist without substances. The following are the qualities.

1 Shape (Rupa)	Physical	Earth, Water and Light
2 Colour (Varna)		Earth, Water and Light
3 Taste (Rasa)		Earth and Water
4 Smell (Gandha)		Earth
5 Touch (Sparsa)		Earth, Water, Light and Air
6 Number (Samkhya)	Numerical	By which we perceive quantity
7 Extension (Parimana)	Relative	
8 Individuality (Pridhaktwa)		
9 Conjunction (Samyoga)		
10 Disjunction (Viyoga)		
11 Priority (Paratwa)		
12 Posteriority (Aparatwa)		

13 Thought (Budhi) 14 Pleasant (Sukha) 15 Pain/sorrow (Dukha) 16 Desire (Icha) 17 Aversion (Dwesha) 18 Will/Effort (prayatna)	Psychological	

Table 3. Qualities of substance - *Padhartha (*Vaisheshika school of thought)

Characteristic and adventitious qualities

A distinction is made afterwards between characteristic and adventitious qualities. If a garment, for instance, is perfumed by a flower, the smell is only an adventitious quality of the garment, while it is characteristic in the case of earth. Thus heat is characteristic of light, cold of water, etc.

3. The actions (Karma)

1. Throwing upward (*Utkshepana*)
2. Throwing downward (*Avakshepana*)
3. Contracting (*Akunchana*)
4. Expanding (*Utsarana /Prasarana*)
5. Going (*Gamana*)

4. **The genus or community (Saamaanya)**

As to *Saamaanya*, the community, or, as we should say, genus, it is supposed to be eternal, and a property common to several, and abiding in substance, in quality, and in action. It is distinguished by degrees, as high and low; the highest *Saamaanya*, or the highest genus (*Jaati*) is *Satta*, mere being, afterwards differentiated by limitations, and developed into ever so many subordinate species.

5. **The species or particularity (Vishesha)**

The single object that which constitutes the individuality or separateness of any object is the species. This also is supposed to abide in eternal substances, so that it seems to have been conceived not as a mere abstraction, but as something real, that was there and could be discovered by means of analysis or abstraction.

6. The inhesion or inseparability (Samavaaya)

It is different from mere conjunction, *Samyoga*, such as obtains between horse and rider, or between milk and water mixed together. There is *Samavaaya* between threads and cloth, between father and son, between two halves and a whole, between cause and effect, between substances and qualities, the two being interdependent and therefore inseparable. The relation between thought and word, for instance, is not *Samyoga*, but *Samavaaya* inseparableness.

7. The negation or privation, or non-existence (Abhaava)

In addition to the above six categories, some logicians required a negative category also, that of *Abhaava* or the absence. There are different kinds of *Abhaava.*

a) *Prag-abhaava*, former non-being, applying to cloth before it was woven

b) *Pradhvamsa*, subsequent non-being, as when a jar, being smashed, exists no longer;

c) *Atyanta-abhaava*, absolute non-being, an impossibility, such as the son of a barren woman

d) *Anyonya-abhaava*, reciprocal negation, or mutual difference, such as we see in the case of water and ice

3. SAMKHYA PHILOSOPHY

The word *Samkhya* means *to know the truth.* This reflects its origin in preliterate systematic theory. Kapila is the founder.

The *rishis* perceived, in close relationship between man and universe, how cosmic energy manifests in all living and non-living things. They also realized that the source of all existence is *cosmic consciousness,* which manifests as male and female energy; *Purusha* is the male while *Prakriti* is the female energy. Purusha is formless, colourless and beyond attributes and takes no active part in the manifestation of the universe. This energy is choice -less passive awareness.

'Prakriti' has form, colour and attributes. It is awareness with choice; it is divine will, the one who designs to become many. The universe is the child born out of the womb of prakriti, the divine mother. Prakriti meets all forms in the universe, while purusha is the witness to this creation. It is the primordial physical energy containing the three attributes or guna, *Satwa, Raja and Tama* found in all nature, the evolving cosmos. The qualities of the three at- tributes are given in the following table.

Satwa	Raja	Tama
Virtue Beautiful, good, wise, Intelligence & self conscious-ness	Passion Active, fierce Energy	Dullness Dark, stupid, ugly Sloth

Table. 4 Attributes of the three basic components of creation

Raja is the active vital life force in the body which moves both organic and inorganic universe to *satwa* and *tamas* respectively. *Satwa* and *Tamas* are inactive potential energies, which needs the active kinetic force of *Raja*.

- Satwa is creative potential
- Rajas the kinetic protective force and
- Thamas is the potential destructive force.

Creation, protection and destruction are the three manifestations of t he 'Supreme cosmic power', which constantly operate the universe.

Each person is composed of Prakriti (gross body) and is simultaneously Purusha (subtle body). But most people cannot see the difference because they are obviously Prakriti in substance. People have the illusion of being Prakriti also in essence. Thus soul is bound to matter. But the soul can know its true nature and find release. Meditation is the key.

When attempting meditation for the first time you will be amazed at how busy your mind is and how easily it slides from sloth to passion to intelligence and back again. Personality and intellect are attributes of matter (Prakriti) and not of spirit (Purusha)

> How we feel is within our power to change
>
> It's our responsibility to create good, positive feelings that make life worth living.
>
> Even the brief, simple procedures of meditation can be very powerful in actually reducing the flow of certain neurotransmitters and stress hormones, an effect that may be mediated by an increased sense of control and mastery.

4. THE PHILOSOPHY OF YOGA

The word Yoga is derived from the Sanskrit root *Yuj* meaning to bind, join, attach and yoke, to direct and concentrate one's attention on, to use and apply. It also means union or communion. It is the true union of our will with the will of God; it means the disciplining of the intellect, the mind, the emotions, the will, which that Yoga presupposes; it means a poise of the soul which enables one to look at life in all its aspects evenly.

Yoga is one of the six orthodox systems of Indian philosophy. It was collated, co-ordinated and systematised by Patanjali in his classical work, the Yoga

Sutras, which consists of 196 terse aphorisms. In Indian thought, everything is permeated by the Supreme Universal Spirit (*Paramatma* or God) of which the individual human spirit (*Jeevatma*) is a part. The system of Yoga is so called because it teaches the means by which the *Jeevatma* can be united to, or be in communion with the Paramatma, and so secure liberation (*Moksha*). One who follows the path of Yoga is a *Yogi* or *Yogin*.

Bhagavad Gita, is the most important authority on Yoga philosophy. Sri Krishna explains to Arjuna the meaning of Yoga as a deliverance from contact with pain and sorrow.

'When his mind, intellect and self (*Ahamkara*) are under control, freed from restless desire, so that they rest in the spirit within, a man becomes a *Yukta* – one in communion with God. A lamp does not flicker in a place where no winds blow; so it is with a yogi, who controls his mind, intellect and self, being absorbed in the spirit within him. When the restlessness of the mind, intellect and self is stilled through the practice of Yoga, the yogi by the grace of the Spirit within himself finds fulfillment. Then he knows the eternal joy, which is beyond the pale of the senses, which his reason cannot grasp. He abides in this reality and moves not there from. He has found the treasure above all others. There is nothing higher than this. He, who has achieved it, shall not be moved by the greatest sorrow.

As a well cut diamond has many facets, each reflecting a different colour of light, so does the word yoga, each facet reflecting a different shade of meaning and revealing different aspects of the entire range of human endeavor to win inner peace and happiness.

The Bhagavad Gita also gives other explanations of the term yoga and lays stress upon Yoga by action (Karma Yoga).

'Work alone is your privilege, never the fruits thereof. Never let the fruits of action be your motive; and never cease to work. Work in the name of the

Lord, abandoning selfish desires. Be not affected by success or failure. This balance of forces or symmetry is called Yoga.'

Yoga has also been described as wisdom in work or skillful living amongst activities, harmony and moderation. Yoga is not for him who gorges too much, nor for him who starves himself. It is not for him who sleeps too much, nor for him who stays awake. By moderation in eating and in resting, by regulation in working and by concordance in sleeping and waking, Yoga destroys all pain and sorrow.

The *Kanthopanishad* describes Yoga like this:

'When the senses are stilled, when the mind is at rest, when the intellect wavers not - then, say the wise, is reached the highest stage. This steady control of the senses and mind has been defined as Yoga. He who attains it is free from delusion.'

In the second aphorism of the first chapter of the Yoga Sutra, Patanjali describes Yoga as '*chitta vrtti nirodhah*'. This may be translated as the restraint (*nirodhah*) of mental (*chitta*) modifications (*vrtti*) or as suppression (*nirodhah*) of the fluctuations (*vrtti*) of consciousness (*chitta*).

The word *chitta* denotes the mind in its total or collective sense as being composed of three categories:

(a) Mind (*mana:*) - the individual mind having the power and faculty of attention, selection and rejection; it is the oscillating indecisive faculty of the mind.

(b) Intelligence or reason (*Buddhi*) - that is, the decisive state which determines the distinction between things, and

(c) Ego (*Ahamkara*) - literally the I-maker, the state, which ascertains that 'I know'.

The word *Vrtti* is derived from the Sanskrit root '*Vrt*' meaning to turn, to revolve, or to roll on. It thus means course of action, behaviour, mode of being, condition or mental state.

Yoga is the method by which the restless mind is calmed and the energy directed into constructive channels. As a mighty river which when properly harnessed by dams and canals, creates a vast reservoir of water, prevents famine and provides abundant power for industry; so also the mind, when controlled, provides a reservoir of peace and generates abundant energy for human uplift.

How Yoga works?

A person's mental and physical health depends on brain and body chemicals. Regular practice of yoga alters the brain chemistry. It slows down the action of the sympathetic nervous system. In practical terms it means that our body do not get flooded with stress hormones as quickly, our blood pressure do not rise every time we have an argument and our heart does not start pounding for fear of missing the bus.

Regular practice of yoga also improves the functioning of Parasympathetic system that controls our ability to relax. Even after a period of stress we are able to relax and normalize quickly.

Tense muscles, send unnecessary stress signals to the brain but once they are gently stretched in yogic postures, the signals are automatically switched off. Over the time Yoga also stimulates sluggish glands into operate more efficiently and chemical balance is restored. That may explain yoga can bring down stress related diabetes, high blood pressure and heart disease.

Samkhya and Yoga share similar thoughts.

In both the ultimate aim is to realise moksha, release or liberation. That is the release from the obscurations caused by mind stuff and sense objects. When we can see through the fog created by the mind and by the senses we can experience our true Self in all its pristine purity. When this happens the world and all our activities appear as a picture show, having no permanent reality. Although we continue to live and act we are no longer involved in it as we were formerly. We are detached because we now understand it.

Emotions are difficult to define and difficult to measure

But we now accept the idea that emotions and other experiences influence people's illness and pattern of recovery.

Stress too, like emotion, is hard to define and hard to quantify.

According to Hans Selye's (1979) stress is the nonspecific response of the body to any demand made upon it. Meditation is the medicine to both.

Psychoneuroimmunology deals with the ways in which the experiences, especially stressful ones alter immune system and how it in turn influences the Central Nervous System

5. MIMAMSA PHILOSOPHY

Mimamsa is a Sanskrit word meaning 'investigation, inquiry, discussion'. It is for 'the investigation of the proper interpretation of the Vedic texts. It is concerned with the earlier or prior section of the Vedas. Therefore it is also called as the 'Poorva mimamsa', or 'it is prior school of investigation'. Dharma is a key word in Mimamsa doctrine, being used in the sense of sacred and moral duties. It also means the virtue obtained by following actions in accord with the dharma. Mimamsa claims that the scriptures are the only way of knowing about dharma, and only by following the scriptures, we can attain dharma as the good.

Dharma might be considered the way of higher truths. It is the way of living. The way to the truth is knowledge.

According to John Locke (1632 –1704), what we know is always properly understood as the relation between ideas. All our ideas – simple or complex- are ultimately derived from experience. The consequence of this empiricist approach is that the knowledge of which we are capable is severely limited in its scope and certainty.

6. THE PHILOSOPHY OF VEDANTA

'Vedanta' is a combination of two words: 'Veda' means knowledge and 'anta' means 'the end of' or 'the goal of.' Here the goal of knowledge is not intellectual - the limited knowledge we acquire by reading books, but knowledge of God as well as the knowledge of our own divine nature. Vedanta, then, is the search for Self-knowledge as well as the search for God.

According to Vedanta, soul is eternal and was never produced or came in to existence at a particular time in the history. It does not die when the body is put to death. The basic foundation of Ayurveda also is the same. Such knowledge (Veda) makes the term "Ayurveda", the knowledge of life. A healthy body is where the soul dwells long! Vedanta is universal in its application and is equally relevant to all countries, all cultures, and all religious backgrounds.

Throughout antiquity and into the Middle Ages there was a nexus between medicine and philosophy. Scientists in the world often were philosophers as well as physicians, and the distinction between the two fields was often blurred. Even in late antiquity, when the philosopher-physician Galen reigned supreme, philosophy was considered a necessary part of medicine training and rational medicine and faith healing existed side by side, never fully divorcing themselves from one another.

The intrusion of hypothetical philosophers in to the medicine cannot be blamed because it was the only means of explaining the cause of diseases; but following the hypotheses still in the medicine can never be justified.

As per the Hindu tradition cutting the dead body was forbidden. Unlike philosophy and medicine, which worked in harmony, the tension between medicine and religious belief often shifted or impeded physiological research.

CHAPTER –2

AYURVEDA - the metaphysical healing system

Covering the six philosophies, we now reached an entrance. 'The Museum of Ayurveda'. There are enough to see ahead where many terminologies may be dusted and allergic! Never get thought blocked in comparison with the current knowledge. Realize the fact that all our current knowledges also would be in archeological galleries in the future!

> Medicine is as old as man and must have come into being with the first awakening of human consciousness. It was practiced by priests who were considered next to only king and the practice itself was a mixture of magic, rites and rituals.
>
> The post 'Upanishad period' (800 BC to 1000 AD) may be considered as 'The golden age of Indian Medicine'.
>
> Ayurveda evolved during this period.

The Origin of Ayurveda

Ayurveda had a divine origin, according to its history. The Creator (Bramha) advised Ayurveda to Daksha. Aswins received it from him and advised to Indra. Seeing the epidemics and health problems among the society great saints like Punarvasu, Dhanwanthari, Bharadwaja, Nimi, Kashyap and Lumbayanan learned Ayurveda from Indra for the benefit of the mankind. Later saints like Agnivesha, Hareetha, Bhela, Mandavya, Susrutha, Charaka and Vagbhata wrote books on Ayurveda.

Ayurveda and Human potential

Ayurveda teaches that man is a microcosm, a universe within himself. He is a child of the cosmic forces of the external environment, the macrocosm. His individual existence is indivisible from the total cosmic manifestation.

It views health and disease in holistic terms taking into consideration the inherent relationship between individual and cosmic spirit, individual and cosmic conscious energy and matter. This is explained by *Tridosha principle* of Ayurveda.

According to Ayurveda every human being has four biological and spiritual instincts

1. Religious
2. Financial
3. Procreation
4. The instinct towards the freedom.

Balanced good health is the foundation for the fulfillment of these instincts

Aayu: kaamayama'anena dharma'artha'sukha'saadhanam'

Ayurvedopadeseshu vidheya: paramadhara. AH (s) 1,2.

Dharma – the individual life purpose

Artham – The financial or material wealth

Sukham (Kaama) – The procreative pleasure

Saadhanam (Sidhi/Moksha) – Freedom, the liberation from the individual 'I' concept.

The unique concept of life in Ayurveda contains two inseparable entities, 'health' and 'intelligence'. We, in pursuing the modern goals of life with *Kaama* (the pleasure) and *Artha* (the material wealth) understand only the need for the health. The true purpose of Ayurveda is to develop intelligence. This 'intelligence' is not the capacity to deal effectively with one's environment or the capacity to think rationally. It is the cellular consciousness that make us aware of our physical body. It is not possible without recognizing *Dharma*, the individual's life purpose and Moksha, the freedom from the individual 'I' concept

The Ayurvedic concept of 'perfect health' is only achieved by carefully following these four spiritual instincts.

The Eight Branches of Ayurveda

Ayurveda, the *metaphysical healing life science*, the mother of all healing arts, is explained in eight branches.

1. Kayachikitsa**:** The Internal medicine**.** This branch deals with treatment of the entire being, mind, body and spirit. It contains an exhaustive list of diseases and herbal medicines, as well as the practice of Pancha Karma.

2. Kaumarabhritya: Paediatrics. All relating to children, including Prenatal, postnatal and childhood diseases are addressed.

3. Graha chikitsa: Psychiatry. Literally means "knowledge of ghosts", *Bhuta-vidya* is related to the treatment of m ental problems using herbs, diet and yoga.

4. Shalakya Tantra: Cover ENT disease and managements. Opthalmology also is included under this heading. Ancient ENT and Opthalmic surgical techniques, follow up and herbal treatments are described.

5. Shalyatantra: Acharya Susrutha's "Susrutha Samhitha" provides ancient surgical techniques and treatments. Use of va rious surgical instruments and procedures are recorded.

6. Agadatantra: Deals with Poisoning and Toxicology. Gradation and treatment of toxins of all sorts, including air and waterborne are explained.

7. Vajikarana: Aphrodisiac, fertility medicines and procedures.

8. Rasayana**:** Rejuvenation**.** Rasayana is used to ensure long, healthy life and prevent disease. It is concerned with healthy diet and code of therapy to impede the degenerative process in the body.

Archeological excavations from the ancient period (3000 BC) show clear evidence of knowledge of comparative anatomy.

The two proponents of Ayurveda who practiced it were Susrutha and Charaka.

Susrutha lived in 2 BC.

Charaka's writings (Charaka samhitha) can be dated back to 1 AD.

During this period, anatomy was studied on dead body

After removing excretes, the body, wrapped in grass and placed in a cage was hidden in river. The thoroughly decomposed body was taken out and slowly scrubbed with a whisk made of grass roots (Kusa) to study the internal parts!

CHAPTER – 3

THE PATHOPHYSIOLOGICAL BASIS OF AYURVEDA

A. TRIDOSHA. (*Vata, Pitha and Kapha*)

The term 'Tridosha' is a composition of two words, 'Tri' meaning three and 'Dhosha', the irreducible physiological principles that regulates the different functions of the body and (mind); the word means 'that which can be vitiated by causes'.

Our body is composed of between 50 to 100 trillion cells. Each cell has a complex structure, which needs a high internal order. This is accomplished by four primary means:

(1). Synthesis of biomolecules (2). Transport of ions and molecules across the cell membranes (3). Production of force and movements and (4). Removal of metabolic waste products and other toxic substances.

Let us see what Ayurveda says about such complex biological needs.

According to Ayurveda, all the bodily functions are believed to be governed by the presence of 3 humours called *vata, pitha and kapha.* They determine the life, health and disease in the body. Homeostasis (*Swastyam*) is the correct balancing between the triad. Disruption of homeostasis result in disturbances of immune mechanisms and it is the primary factor in the etiology of diseases.

VATA IS DESTRUCTIVE
KAPHA CONSTRUCTIVE
AND
PITHA BEING ENERGYIS THE STIMULATOR

Why only 'three principles' (the tridosha)? Where did it come from?

Rig Veda contains verses on the nature of health and disease and discusses the concept of three dosha -Vata, Pitha and Kapha. Ancient Ayurvedic acharyas (scientists) comprehended their observations on the basis of fore-said philosophies and tried to explain health, diseases and treatments using *tridosha.* Without any change or updates even now physiology, pathophysiology, pharmacology and treatments in Ayurveda are based on this humoral principles. It is true that no other conservative parameters, if any, can be as beautiful as the 'concept' of Tridosha to explain the body functions. Thus tridosha is the portrait of Ayurveda.

Dosha have no physical existence; it is a hypothesis. The number 'three' is very important and can be compared to a tripod, which is never balanced if any of the legs are altered. Some philosophers included '*Shonitha'* (Blood) as the fourth Dosha. But is not accepted in Ayurveda as a Dosha.

Qualities (guna) of Tridosha

Specific qualities of each dosha are responsible for the physiological, pathological and pharmacological functions. See the table below.

Vata qualities		Pitha qualities		Kapha qualities	
Sanskrit	English	Sanskrit	English	Sanskrit	English
Rooksha	Dry	Sneha	Fatty	Snigdha	Oily
Laghu*	Light	Theekshna	Potent	Sheetha**	Cold
Sheetha**	Cold	Ushna	Hot	Guru	Heavy
Khara	Solid	Laghu*	Light	Manda	Sluggish
Sookshma	Micro	Visra	Purulent (Spreading)	Slashma	Viscous
Chala	Moving	Sara	Spreading	Mritsna	Pasty
		Drava	Liquid	Sthira	Stationary

* Laghu (light) is common to Vata and Pitha. ** Sheetha (cold) is common to Vata and Kapha

Table 5. Qualities of tridosha

Karma (physiological activity) of Tridoshas

All though they regulates thousands of separate functions in the body and mind their basic functions are:

1. VATA

Utsaahochwaasa niswaasa, cheshta, vegapravarthanai:

Samyaggathya cha dhaathoonaam, askhaanampaadavena cha

Anugrahnathyavikritha Chala: (A.H.S)

Happiness (action on mind), Inspiration and expiration (respiration), neuromuscular activities, normal excretions of the wastes, normal metabolism forming the healthy tissues of all sorts (Saptha dhaatu), normal function of the eyes and other sense organs with the proper association of their objects (*Indriyartha)* are achieved by the non-vitiated Vata.

Thus Vata represents the motion and flow.

2. PITHA *Anugrahnathi avikritha: Pitham pakthy, ooshma darsnai:*

Kshuth, thrit, ruchi, prabha, medha, dhee, saurya, thanu, mardhava:

Digestion, regulation of body temperature, visual power (comparable to the function of rods and cones), appetite, thirst, taste, fairness (body colour, comparable to the proper skin pigmentation), consciousness, cleverness, courage, and body softness are all achieved by the non-vitiated Pitha.

Thus Pitha directs all the metabolic activities, energy exchange and digestion.

3. KAPHA *(avikritha) Sleshma: sthirathwa, snigdhathwa, sandhibandha-kshamaadhibhi:*

The body stability, oilness, articulation of joints, strength all are determined by the non-vitiated Kapha.

Thus Kapha represents structure, cohesion and fluid balance of the body.

Alcmaeon, a Greek philosopher (500 BC) was one of Hippocrate's (the father of modern medicine, born in the island of Cos about 460 BC and died about 377 BC) predecessors. He placed the seat of intelligence in the brain and was the first to excise the human eye. By tracing the optic nerves to the chiasma he recognized the basis of binocular vision.

He was probably the first physician to formulate the doctrine of health as a balance among the powers of the body, these powers being constituent fluids with definite qualities and casual properties. When one dominated over another illness developed. Hippocrates modified this later to the Theory of Four Humours (liquid) - Blood, Yellow and Black bile and the phlegm, which was the basis of medical theory for a long period. The humours are associated with four elements (air, fire, earth and water), which in turn corresponded each to a pair of qualities (hot, cold, dry and moist). Thus also was temperament – sanguine (blood), choleric (yellow bile), melancholic (black bile) or phlegmatic (phlegm) – of body or mind supposed to be determined.

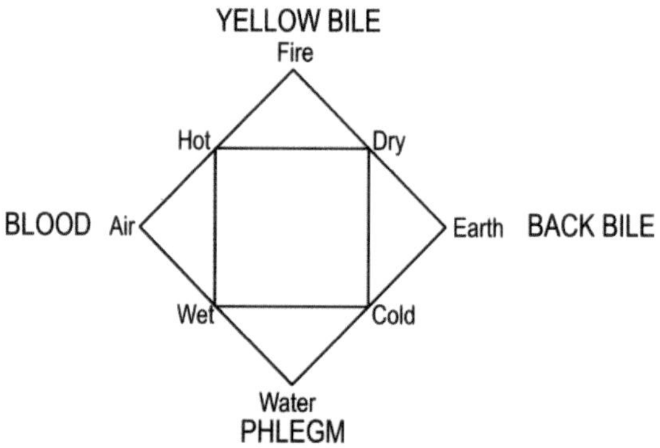

Distribution and specific area of action of tridosha

The action of tridosha is based on three areas of the body. See the table 6 below. It doesn't mean that they are inert in other areas.

1. The systems in the body (*Ashaya*).
2. Tissues (*dhathu*)
3. Sense organs (*Indriya*)

Doshas	Systems	Tissues	Sense organs
Vata	Large intestine	Bones (Vertebral column) ? ref to brain & spinal cord	Auditory and tactile
Pitha	Stomach and digestive	Blood	Visual and tactile
Kapha	Stomach and respiratory	Muscle, fat, marrow Reproductive tissues	Olfactory and taste

Table. 6. Physiologically acting areas of tridosha

Subdivisions of Tridosha

A state of relative constancy of the internal environment of the body is known as homoeostasis, and it is maintained according to Ayurveda by the effectors that are regulated by Vata, Pitha and Kapha; each having five subunits. Thus total of fifteen. Each one has an area of existence, area of distribution for its actions, control on specific organs and their activities. This is how Ayurveda explain the physiology.

Modern Physiology is the study of the biological function - of how the body works from cell to tissue, tissue to organ, organ to system and how the organism as a whole accomplishes particular tasks essential for life.

Dosha	Sub divisions				
Vata	Prana	Udana	Vyana	Samana	Apana
Pitha	Paachaka	Ranjaka	Sadhaka	Alochaka	Brajaka
Kapha	Avalambaka	Kledaka	Bodhaka	Tharpaka	Sleshmaka

Table. 7 Subdivisions of Tridosha (3 x 5 = 15)

Dosha	Location	Distribution	Control	Activity
1.Prana	Head (Brain)	Thorax & throat (trachea & lungs)	Consciousness, mind, heart & sense organs	Spitting, sneezing, belching, respiration & swallowing
2.Udana	Throat	Nose, throat and navel	Life (Prana)	Speech, activity, freshness, strength, Complexion & memory.
3.Vyana	Heart	Whole body	Circulation	All neuromuscular activities like walking, turning & blinking
4.Samana	Duodenum	G.I system	Peristalsis	Digestion, absorption, formation of stool and peristalsis
5.Apana	Rectum	Sacrum, Urinary bladder, Genital organ and thigh	Excretion and Parturition	Defecation, Urination, Menstruation, Ejaculation & labor

Table. 8 Divisions of Vata showing location, distribution, control and activity

Vata functions can be related to the neurological functions including that of Central nervous system, Peripheral nervous system, Myenteric and Myocardial electrical potential and generation.

Dosha	Location	Distribution	Control	Activity
1.Pachaka (Jadaragni)	Duodenum	Middle of the abdomen	Digestion	Activities of the digestive en-zymes
2.Ranjaka	Stomach	Rasa (Chyme)	Blood	Blood colour, Hemopoieis*
3.Sadhaka	Heart	Heart (seat of mind)	Mind	Achievements with cleverness, consciousness, Proud
4.Alochaka	Eyes	Eye and optic nerve	Vision	Identification and resolution of images
5.Brajaka	Skin	Skin layers	Skin colour	Determine skin complexion

Table. 9 (Divisions of Pitha showing location, distribution, control and activity)

*Ranjaka pitha gives the red colour to the blood. The formation of bl ood (hemopoiesis) or haemoglobin may be the indication. Chyme, the food mixture in the stomach where the Ranjaka pitha is prominent, contains the nutrients needed for the formation of blood and other tissues.

Dosha	Location	Distribution	Control	Activity
1.Avalambaka	Thorax	*Heart, Sacrum	Circulation ?Lymphatic	Basis and strength for all Kapha, heart and lumboscrum
2.Kledaka	Stomach	Stomach lining	Mucosa	Maintain stomach lining with mucous to balance the acidity during digestion
3.Bhodaka	Tongue	Taste buds	Taste	Identify tastes
4.Tharpaka	Head (frontal)	Sinuses	Senses	Proper function of ocular & olfactory sense organs
5.Sleshmaka	Joints	Sinovial joints	Lubrication	Maintain synovial joint, structure/function

Table. 10 Division of kapha showing location distribution, control and activity

*The description of *Avalambaka kapha* never seems to be blood related. More over Kapha dosha alone is never blood in nature unless it is not strongly associated with pitha. The description of *Avalambaka kapha* distribution is closely related to path of the thoracic duct (for lymphatic circulation.)

Thoracic duct the 'van Hoorner's canal or Pecquest's duct' is the largest lymph vessel in the body beginning at the cysterna chyli at about the level of second lumbar vertebra, it passes through the aortic opening of the diaphragm, crosses the posterior mediastinum, and discharges into the left brachiocephalic vein at its origin.

Relative influence of Dosha in the body

Factors that influence the status of dosha in the body are: Age, Day, Night and Food in the stomach.

Kapha stage: (1) child hood, (2) first one-third of the day (3) first one third of the night and (4) initial stage of food in the stomach.

Pitha stage: (1) the youth (2) middle one third of the day (3) middle one third of the night, and (4) digesting stage of the food.

Vata Stage: (1) old age (2) the last one third of the day (3) last one third of the night and (4) the post-digested period of the food in the stomach.

Factors	Dosha prominence		
	Vata	Pitha	Kapha
Age	Old Age	Youth	Childhood
Day	Last one-third	Middle one-third	First one-third
Night	Last one-third	Middle one-third	First one-third
Food	After digestion	During digestion	Before digestion

Table. 11. Relative prominence of tridosha in the body

PRAKRITHI (The genetic types)

(The genetic transmission – formation of the types)

During fertilization, tridosha contained in the genetic materials make seven types of combinations known as '*Prakrithi*' (The Natural Types). These are *congenital types* and are named after the prominent single dosha or dosha combinations.

<u>Seven types of constitutions (*Saptha Prakrithi*)</u>

1. Sama prakrithi (Perfect type). Only one type.
2. Eka dosha prakriti (Single dosha prominent combination). Three types
3. Dvanda prikriti (Two dosha prominent combination). Three types.

Three dosha in equal proportions makes a *'Sama prakrtithi'* (Perfect type). Single dosha prominent combination is named on its name, like Vata prominent as Vata type, Pitha prominent as Pitha type and Kapha prominent as Kapha type.

Equally elevated two dosha combinations make a binary group like, Vata - Pitha type, Pitha-Kapha type, and Kapha-Vata type.

Except 'Sama prakrithi' (the perfect type), all other combinations are considered imperfect. Such are hereditary combinations, hence natural! They are characteristically normal individuals. It is like poison in the poisonous animals where their poison is not harmful to themselves! (Don't confuse such *'imperfects'* are poisonous to others! The example is a comparison given in Ayurvedic text –A.H Su 1/10). But any pathologically acquired imperfect combinations of tridosha in the gametes presumably create consequences.

In all the seven types, dosha vitiation can pathologically occur during spermatogenesis (meosis), oogenesis (meosis), cleavage (mitosis) or at any stages of development of the foetus. The very poor combinations may not result in fertilization or may cause abortion. In survived cases foetal abnormalities can occur.

No	Combinations	Prakrithi	Quality grading
1	Equal	Sama prakriti	Perfect
2	Kapha high	Kapha prakriti	Best
3	Pitha high	Pitha prakriti	Medium
4	Vata high	Vata prakriti	Poor
5	Kapha –Pitha	Kapha-Pitha prakriti	Bad
6	Vata-Kapha	Vata-Kapha prakriti	Bad
7	Vata-Pitha	Vata-Pitha prakriti	Bad

Table. 12 Qualitative representation of the seven congenital types

DOSHA DUSHTI

(The vitiation and pathological manifestation of dosha)

Vitiation means '*to reduce the value or quality of; impair or spoil'*. According to Ayurveda the important criterion of health is '*stable tridosha*'. This refers to a state of *homeostasis*, the tendency towards a relatively stable equilibrium between the interdependent elements, especially as maintained by physiological processes.

'*Dosha dushti*' creates an '*impaired proportion of tridosha*; a destabilized equilibrium developing to etiological condition. Pathological manifestation starts thereafter.

The study of '*science and specialty practice*' that deals with all aspects of disease, but with special reference to the essential nature, the causes, and the development of the abnormal conditions as well as structural and functional changes that result from the disease processes is called as pathology.

Tridosha do not have a physical existence; though a combination of *Panchamahabhoota* which exists physically it fails to show a structural view for tridosha. In this chapter, for an easy perception I structuralized them in coloured columns of graphic representation.

Vitiation of dosha is the change in their integrity, due to any cause(s) that may be intimate, non-intimate or instrumental. According to Ayurveda the intimate cause of disease is always the vitiated dosha. Beware, *dosha dushti* is not as such a disease, it is etiological only. Different causes vitiate tridosha, as discussed in Chapter 4.

Classification of cause, the modern concept.

1. *Constitutional cause*: Cause acting within or through some systemic process or inborn error.
2. *Exciting cause*: The direct provoking cause of a disease
3. *Predisposing cause*: Anything that produces a susceptibility or disposition to disease without itself causing the disease.
4. *Proximate cause*: The immediate actual cause.
5. *Specific cause*: One, the action of which produces only one definite disease.

   Eg. The specific microorganism causing diphtheria, tuberculosis or tetanus.

Dosha can be vitiated together or individually. Both are pathological. When single dosha is vitiated the symptoms of that dosha is manifested. In case of dual dosha vitiation the combined symptoms of the two are presented.

Vata vitiated symptoms	Pitha vitiated symptoms	Kapha vitiated symptoms
All kinds of pain	Burning sensation	Oily
Numbness	Reddishness	Hardening
Fatigue	Heat	Itching
Cramps	Inflammation	Chillness
Thirst	Sweating	Heaviness
Tremor	Seborrhea	Obstruction
Dryness	Oozing	Adiposis
Perforation	Decay	Inactivity
Emaciation	Disintegration	Oedema
Tingling	Coma	Indigestion
Girdle pain	Disorientation	Hypersomnia
Malfunctions	Hot and acidic taste	Pallor
Sour mouth	Discolouration except	Sweet and Salty
Blemishes	white and pink	Chronicity
Erythema		

Table. 13 General symptoms of each vitiated dosha

'Vayu: pitham kaphaschethi thrayo Doshassamaasatha:
prathyekam they thridha vridhi,kshaya,saamya,vibhedatha:
akrishta,Madhya,alpathaya thridha vridhi,kshayavapi......'

Vata, Pitha and Kapha can be vitiated individuallyin two types.
Vridhi (by increase), 2. Kshaya (by decrease)
Both of these can be presented in three types

Type 1: a) Highly increased, b) Medium increase, c) Little increased

Type 2: a) Highly decreased, b) Medium decrease, c) Little decreased

TYPES OF VITIATION

Please note that the colours used for representing the dosha are only for illustration.

I. Doshas vitiated individually. In following SIX types

1. Vata vitiation (in all graphs below the blue line is to show the normal status)

(a) Increase: **(i)** Vata dosha increased, Pitha and Kapha not affected

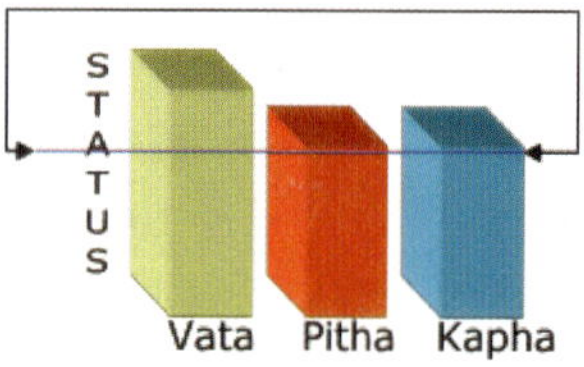

Symptoms

1. Weight lose
2. Blackening (Skin)
3. Desire forhot
4. Tremor
5. Flatulence
6. Constipation
7. Fatigue
8. Insomnia
9. Weakness (diseases) of sense organs
10. Delirium
11. Giddiness, and
12. Weak appearance (? emaciated)

Vata vitiation

(b) Decrease

(ii) Vata dhosha decreased, Pitha and kapha not affected

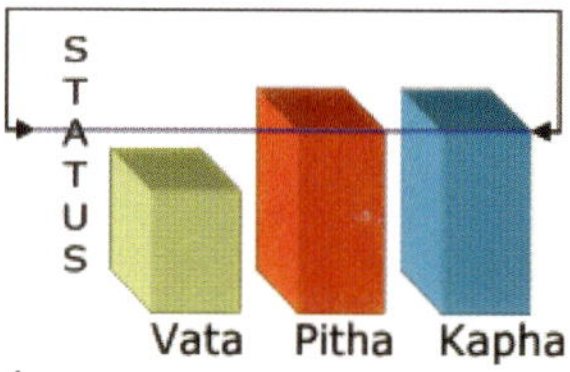

Symptoms

1. Wasting
2. Dysarthria and ataxia
3. Loss of motor activity, and
4. The symptoms of increased kapha dosha.

2. Pitha vitiation

(a) Increase

(ii) Pitha dosha increased, Vata and Kapha not affected

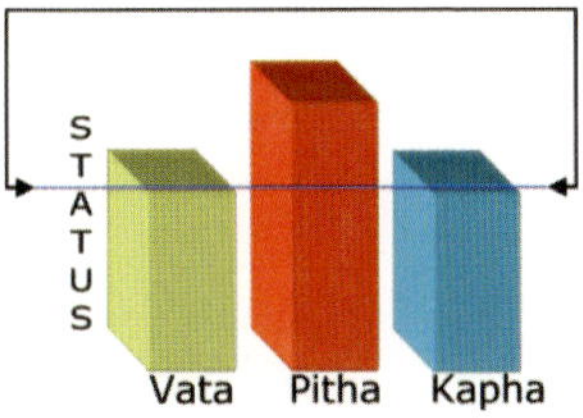

Symptoms

1. Yellowish stool, urine, eyes and skin (? Jaundice)
2. Increased appetite
3. Thirst
4. Burning (? paresthesia), and
5. Insomnia

Pitha vitiation

(b) Decrease

(ii)) Pitha dosha decreased, Vata and Kapha not affected

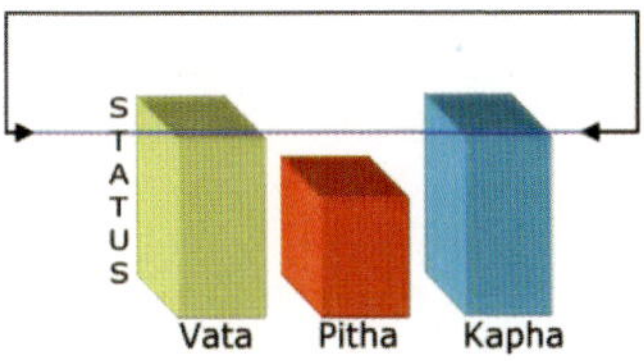

Symptoms

1. Indigestion
2. Coldness (? hypothermia)
3. Reduced glamour (pale look)

3. Kapha vitiation

(a) Increased

(ii) Kapha increased, Vata and Pitha not affected

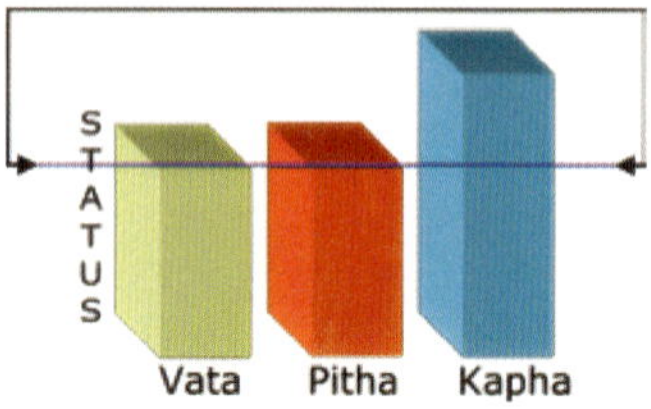

Symptoms

1.	Indigestion
2.	Salivation
3.	Laziness
4.	Heaviness in the body
5.	Paleness
6.	Chillness
7.	Flaccid limbs
8.	Asthama
9.	Cough
10.	Hypersomnia

Kapha vitiation

(b) Decreased

(ii) Kapha decreased, Vata and Pitha not affected

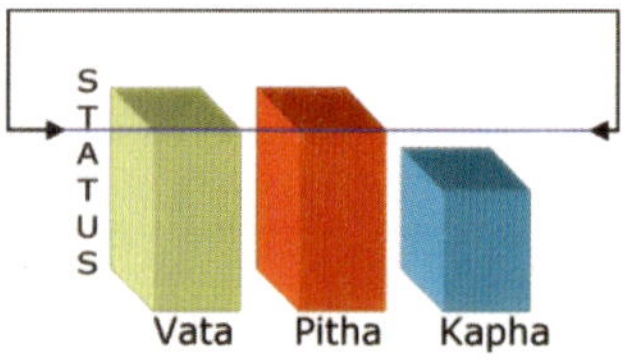

Symptoms

1.	Giddiness
2.	Emptiness of 'kaphashaya' (See table 10)
3.	Chest distress
4.	Flaccid joints

In high, medium and low degree of vitiations the intensity of symptoms will vary accordingly.

II. <u>Dual (two dosha) vitiation.</u> This is called as ***'Samsarga'***

> '***Samsarga****ssannipaathascha thad dwithrischayakopatha:'*
>
> *Thou shoda dashadha chokthavuthkarshadi vikalpanath'* (A.S.S Chapter.1)
>
> Dual dosha vitiation is **Samsarga,** it occurs either by increase or decrease oftwo doshas.
>
> This derangement is presented in THREE groups of SIX each.

There are three types of dual dosha vitiations:

1. Vata-Pitha (Six types from nine patterns)
2. Vata-Kapha (Six types from nine patterns)
3. Pitha-Kapha (Six types from nine patterns)

In the following graphs, SIX types contain NINE patterns of vitiated combinations.

V, P and K represent Vata, Pitha and Kapha.

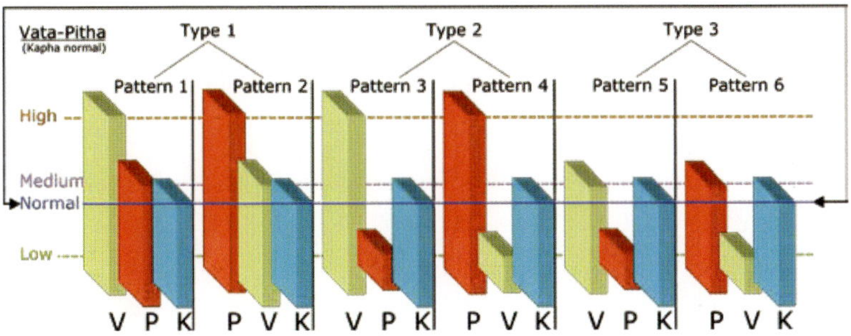

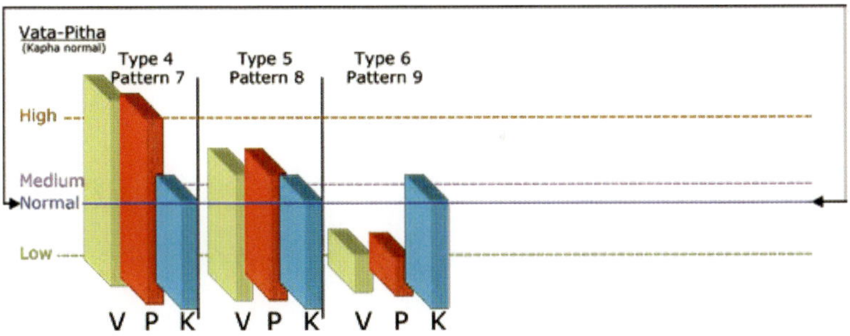

Let us examine how the nine patterns are possible.

In binary vitiation, it occurs either by increase or decrease of two dosha from their normal status (represented by a blue line). Note that here (in samsarga) one dosha maintains the normal level always. Thus possibilities of dual combination are as follows:

1. One dosha highly increased, other medium increase (one with each) — 2 patterns

2. One dosha highly increased, other reduced from normal (one with each) — 2 patterns

3. One dosha medium increase, other reduced from normal (one with each) — 2 patterns

4. Both dosha highly increased only — 1 pattern

5. Both dosha with medium increase only — 1 pattern

6. Both reduced from normal only — 1 pattern

Note that only in 4th and 5th types the clinical symptoms vary only in strength. Other types are obviously presented with unique symptoms.

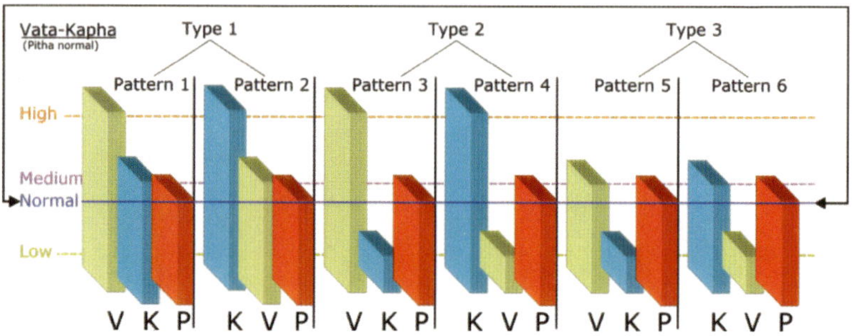

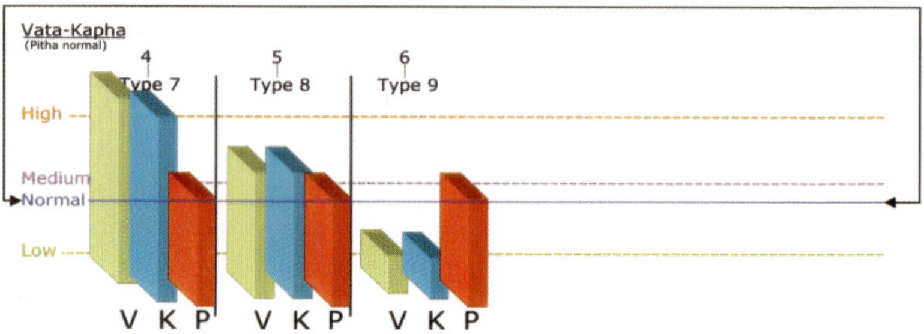

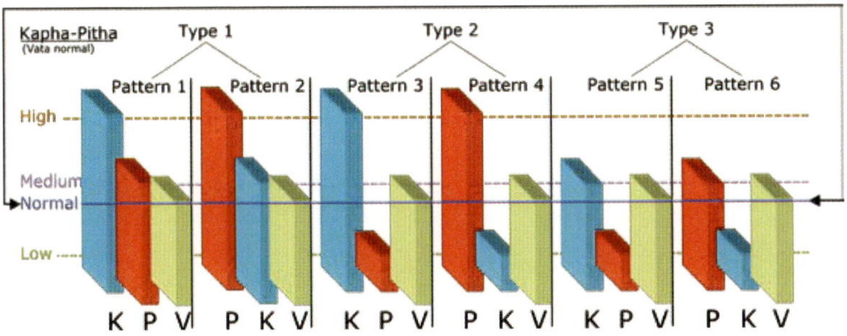

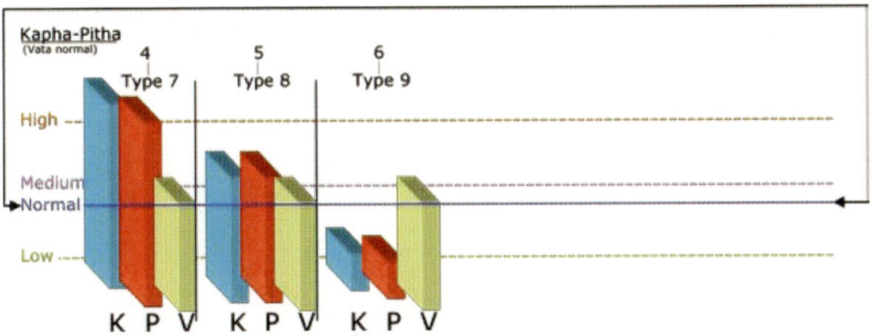

III. **Three doshas vitated together**. This is called as ***Sannipatha***

*Samsargas**sannipatha**scha thadwithrischayakopatha:' Thou shoda*, **dasha**dha *chokthavuthkarshadi vikalpanath'* (A.S.S Chapter.1)

'Dasha' = Ten

When three doshas are vitiated together it is called *Sannipatha*. It is presented in TEN types, from TWENTY FOUR patterns.

Three doshas vitiated together (***Sannipatha)***

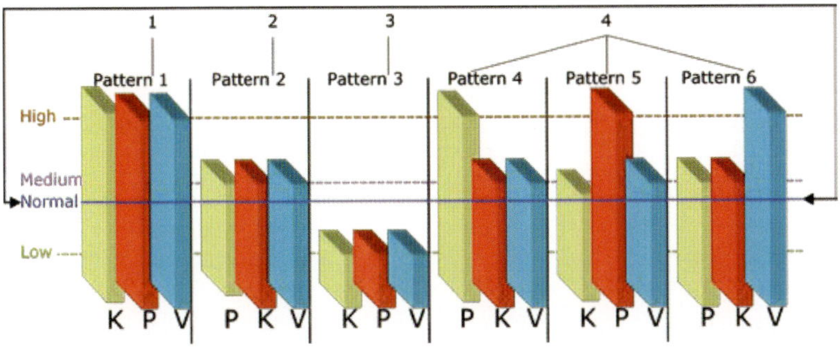

Three doshas vitiated together (***Sannipatha)*** – continued

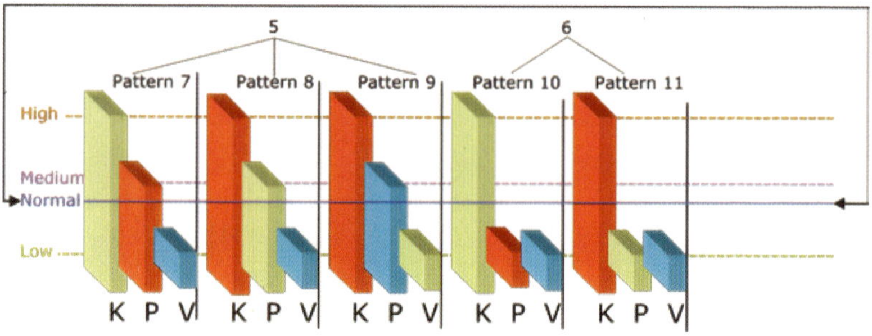

Three doshas vitiated together (***Sannipatha)*** continued

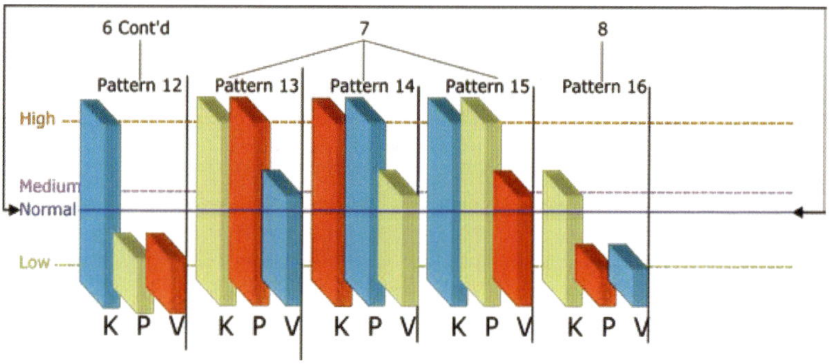

Three doshas vitiated together (***Sannipatha)*** continued

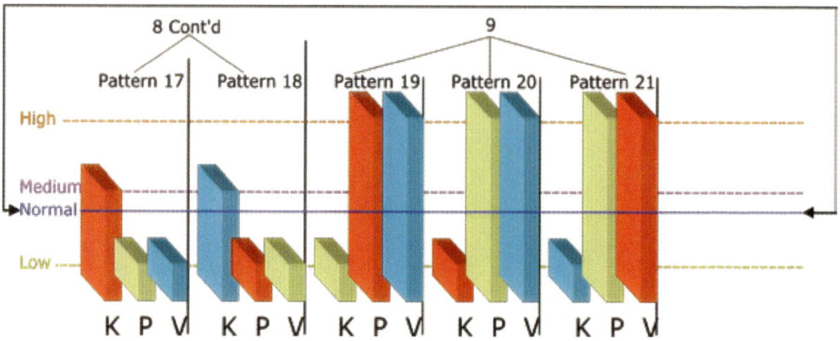

Three doshas vitiated together (***Sannipatha)*** cont'd

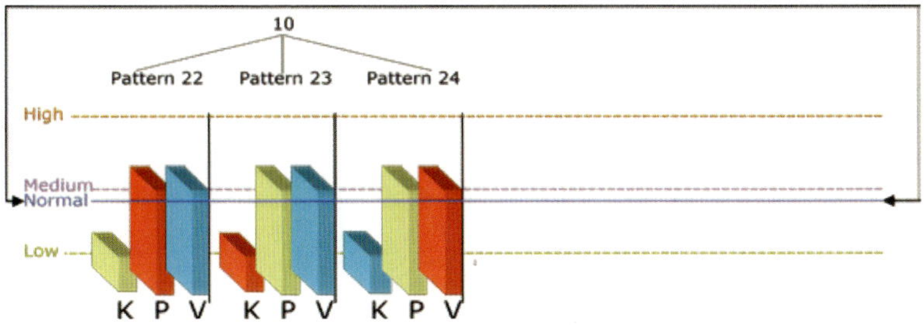

DOSHA BASED CLINICALLY VARIENT DISEASE

Dosha vitiation is not 'disease specific'; it is common to all diseases. A given disease may be presented in seven types. The pathological manifestation of a disease occurs according to the type of v itiatied dosha or i ts combination; clinical symptoms also vary accordingly. Same is the situation with prognosis also.

Consider the seven 'Prakrithi' (type) of m an that we have discussed earlier. Each of t hem presents the clinical symptoms of diseases in varied forms, in terms of their 'doshic type'. This diversity insist on the specificity of choosing the drug for the treatment. Ayurveda teach to select the drug to correct vitiated dosha! So same disease need different medicines according to dosha vitiation and type of the patient.

It had become a sort of s edutive doctrine, even among the young generation who enter to Ayurveda with their basic advanced science education to explain any disease, known or unknown with *Tridosha principle*! In fact, I consider it more theoretical and difficult to adopt in general practice. The essential concepts of d isease processes cannot be explained in this way. An incredible amount of medical information is available now for learning pathophysiology. Irrespective of the system of medicine this basic knowledge is compulsory for a medical student. I found c ure in my patients more easily with Ayurvedic medicines when diagnosed using modern parameters.

Disease develops when significant changes occur in the body leading to a state in which homeostasis cannot be maintained. Under normal conditions, homeostasis, or a relatively constant or stable internal environment is maintained within the body with regard to such factors as blood pressure, body temperature, and fluid balance. As frequent minor changes occur in the body, compensation mechanisms respond, and homeostasis is quickly restored. Usually the individual is neither aware of these changes nor the compensations taking place.

A state of health is difficult to define because the genetic differences among the individuals as well as the many variations in life experiences and environmental influences create a variable base.

Pathophysiology involves the study of functional or physiologic changes in the body that result from disease process. To understand this a current knowledge of physiology is absolutely important.

A conceptual approach to explain a 'Science of health' cannot be infallible

B. SAPTHA DHAATU

'Dhaatu' are building blocks (tissues) of the body. A collection of similar cells and the intercellular substances surrounding them are called tissues. Ayurveda explained seven dhaatu. (Saptha means seven)

1. Rasa dhaatu - Chyme
2. Raktha dhaatu - Blood
3. Mamsa dhaatu - Muscular tissue
4. Medha dhaatu - Adipose tissue
5. Asthi dhaatu - Bone tissue
6. Majja dhaatu - Bone marrow
7. Sukra dhaatu - Semen/reproductive tissue

A dhaatu can form only from a precursor. Food is the source of Rasa dhaatu. Others are formed by the successive transition from the one before. The progressive formation without any obstruction in their transformation is necessary for the homeostasis. Each dhaatu has specific energy (*dhaatwagni*) for converting to the next. The precursor should be healthy and the energy for its transformation to the next also should be adequate.

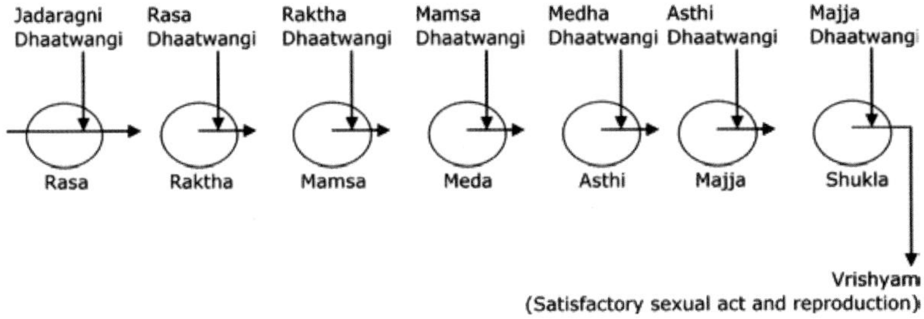

Dhaatu is also known as '*Dhooshya*' because they can be vitiated (structurally and functionally to cause diseases) by the vitiated dosha.

The following table is a comparative approach to each 'dhaatu' with the modern terminology.

No	Sanskrit name	English Name
1	Rasa dhaatu	Chyme (Semifluid mass of partly digested food passed from stomach to duodenum)
2	Raktha dhaatu	Blood (Circulating tissue of the body. Consists of pale yellow or grey yellow fluid, the plasma with suspended red cells, white cells and platelets)
3	Mamsa dhaatu	Muscular tissue (Bundles of reddish fibres, endowed with property of contractility). Two types: Voluntary '*stripped*' and involuntary, '*unstripped*'. Muscular fibres of the heart differ from this structure and is called as cardiac muscular fibres
4	Medha dhaatu	Adipose tissue- (A greasy, soft-solid material found in animal tissues and many plants). Fat is said to be detected in the human embryo about the fourteenth week. Fat cells are formed by the transformation of connective tissue corpuscles.
5	Asthi dhaatu	Bone Tissue (One of the hardest structures of the animal body, possess certain degrees of toughness and elasticity; composed of two types of tissues: dense one called as *compact tissue* and other slender fibers and lamellae forming reticular structure called as *cancellous tissue*)
6	Majja dhaatu	Bone marrow (The soft, fatty substance filling the medullary cavities and cancellous extremities of long bones. Differs in composition in different bones. All blood cells originate from the red bone marrow. In the adult, red bone marrow is in the flat and irregular bones, ribs, vertebrae, ternum and pelvis)
7	Shukra dhaatu	Reproductive tissue (The procreative or potential product both for male and female, responsible for the survival of the species)

Table. 14 A comparative approach to each dhaatu with modern terminology

Karma (functions) of dhaatu

Dhaatu hold the entire body in proper form. The weakness of any one of them affect formation and existence of the following and is pathological. Specific functions are assigned to each as listed below.

(1) Rasa - *Preenana* (Satisfaction)

(2) Raktha -*Jeevana* (Maintain life)

(3) Mamsa - *Lepana* (Attachment)

(4) Medha - *Snehana* (Oiling)

(5) Asthi - *Dhaarana* (Holding)

(6) Majja - Poorana (Filling)

(7) Sukra - *Garbhotpadana* (Procreation)

Dhaatu	Functions – interpreted with current knowledge
Rasa (Chyme)	**Satisfaction** – May be reffering to 'satiation'. The state produced by having a specific need fulfilled, such as hunger or thirst
Raktha (Blood)	**Life** - Blood is the means by which oxygen and nutritive materials are transported to the tissues and carbon dioxide and various metabolic products removed for excretion. Improper blood function is life threatening.
Mamsa (Muscular tissue)	**Attachment -** Proper attachment of bones to form joints is accomplished by muscles; the structure and dynamogenic activities like gross and precise movements need proper muscular design and attachment
Medha (Adipose tissue)	**Oiling** – This fatty layer in the body has many regulatory functions, on the metabolism, body weight, temperature etc. A regulatory molecule produced by the adipocytes is tumor necrosis factor –alpha (TNF*a*). It is good to maintain the set point of adipose tissue, 'The *adipostasis*'
Asthi (Bone)	**Holding.** The main architecture of the body is with the bone. The bone also should be healthy with proper mineralization, strong enough to withstand the stress and strain by the heavy muscular movements.
Majjah (Bone marrow)	**Filling.** Fills up the cylindrical cavity in the shaft of the long bones and occupies spaces of the cancellous tissue and extends into the larger bony canals – *Haversian* Canals.
Shukra (Reproductive tissue)	**Procreation:** This is accomplished by the union of male and female gametes. The *final dhaatu* should be perfectly formed through the previous six, for a normal conception.

Table. 15 Functions of *dhaatu*

VITIATION OF DHAATU

Dhaatu are also called '*dhaatwahara*', the previous one being the *food* for the next during the orderly progression. *Dosha* vitiate *dhaatu* which become pathological in two ways.

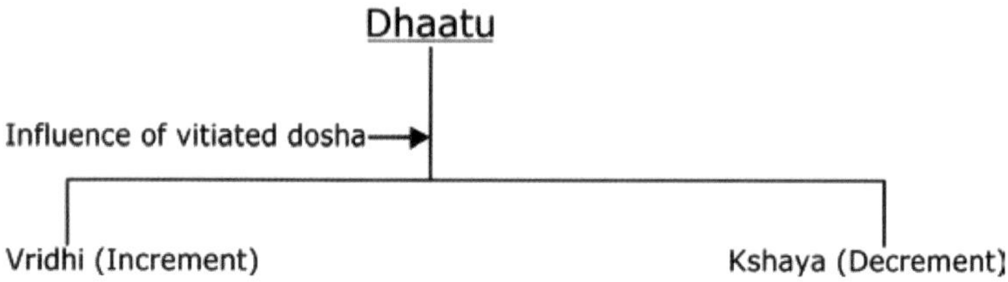

Clinical symptoms

(With Corresponding modern terminology)

Dhaatu	Symptoms in Vridhi (Increment)	Symptoms in Kshaya (Decrement)
Rasa (Chyme)	Symptoms of Kapha dosha increment	Dryness, giddiness, weakness, fatigue, irritations on perceiving sounds.
Raktha (Blood)	Dermatitis, Splenomegaly, Abscess, skin disease, Arthritis, thrombocytopathy, intestinal disorders, pyorrhea, jaundice, blackening on face, indigestion, syncope, hemangioma, redness of eyes, hematuria.	Affinity to acidic substances and cold, vasoparesis, rough skin
Mamsa (Muscular tissue)	Glandular growth, tumour, nodes, Fatty cheeks, thighs, abdomen, neck, exilla etc.	Weakness, wasting and Arthralgia
Medha (Adipose tissue)	Symptoms of Mamsa increase with tiredness, panting on exertion, Steatopygia, macromastia, Panniculus	Numbness around waist, splenomegaly, emaciated limbs
Asthi (Bone)	Exostosis, Peridens	Bone pain, osteoporosis, brittle nail and hair
Majja (Bone marrow)	Heaviness in eyes, limbs, erythematous stubborn ulcers in joints	Osteoporosis, giddiness, blurred vision
Shukra (Reproductive tissue)	Excessive sexual desire, Urolithiasis	Delayed ejaculation, bleeding, scrotal pain and burning genitals

Table 16 Clinical symptoms of vitiated to dhaatu

C. MALA (Excretions of the body)

Abnormal functions of e xcretory systems are considered pathological. GI system, Urinary system and skin are discussed under this heading.

STOOL: Consists primarily of fiber and other indigestible material, sloughed mucosal cells and bacteria. Ayurveda specifically consider the bowel habit in most of t he diseases, emphasizing gastro intestinal tract as the seat of all diseases.

URINE: Nitrogen is ingested primarily as proteins, enters the body as amino acids, and is excreted mainly as urea in the urine. Without the knowledge of amino acid metabolism, mechanism of glomerular filtration, influence of Diuretic hormone (DH) and Anti-diuretic hormone (ADH) Ayurveda considered differences in 'amount of urine, flow, colour, smell and taste as signs of diseases. For example, *Madhumeha* (Glycoseurea) was diagnosed by observing ants attracted to urine.

SWEAT: The fluid excreted by sweat glands, consists of w ater containing sodium chloride and phosphate, urea ammonia, ethereal sulfates, creatinine, fats and other waste products. Sweating plays a great role in the temperature regulation of the body.

'Swedana', the process of i nducing sudation (sweating), is an important detoxifying method in Ayurveda treatment, commonly used as a procedure in *'Panchakarma'*.

All excretions within the limits of t heir quantity and quality is the sign of normal function of t he excretory systems. Vitiated *Dosha* also spoil *mala* which is expressed in deviated normal specifications. So *mala*, like *dhaatu* is also called as *dhooshya* (being vitiated).

Vitiation occurs in two types.

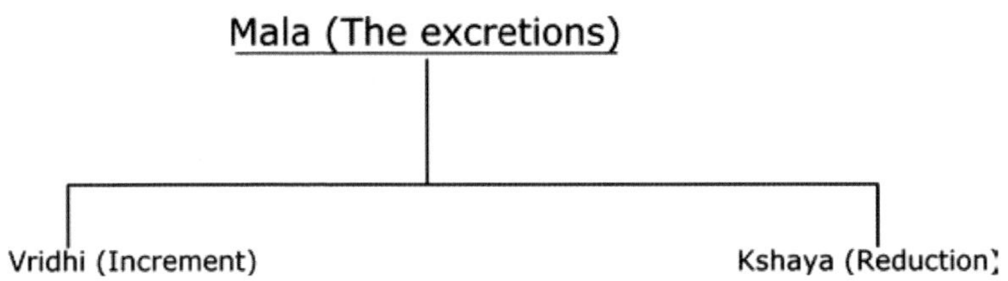

Mala	On Vridhi	On Kshaya
Stool	Flatulence, Borborygmi, abdominal pain and heaviness	Bloating, noisy gas, intra-abdominal pressure with pain on left side of chest, severe belching
Urine	Pain in the bladder and frequent urination	Dysurea, colour change, occasional hematuria
Sweat	Sensible perspiration, bad smell, itching	Hair loss, erectile hairs, cracks on skin

Table 17 Clinical symptoms of vitiated *mala*

The interdependence between dosha, dhaatu and mala

While discussing etiopathology we considered *dosha, dhaatu* and *mala* separately. Knowledge of t heir interdependence is important in *'doshic pathology'*. The concept of dos ha is philosophical. Let us assume that they are *'invisibly existing'*. According to some interpreters, they '*exist at quantum levels'*. A quantum is defined as the basic unit of matter or energy in the form of ten million to hundred million times smaller than the smallest atom.

Dhaatu and *mala* are very obvious structures. They are under the influence of invisible dosha. The influence and conditions of dosha (whether normal or vitiated) are perceived from the conditions of dha atu and mala. Being assumed these conditions let us see how each dosha anchors a particular group of dhaatu and mala, and vice versa. Hope the following illustration can help to explain this.

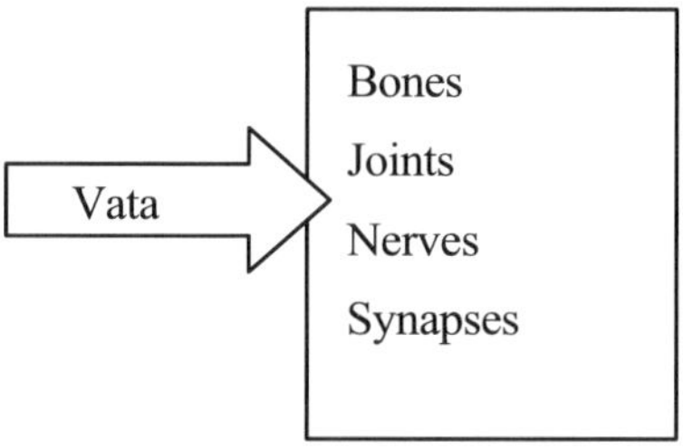

This diagram represents that vata stays in bones, joints, nerves and synapses. Joints, nerves and synapses are not mentioned with sapta dhaatu (table 11). The bones make stable joints with muscles, tendons, blood and nerves supply; Synapses is a part of nerves.

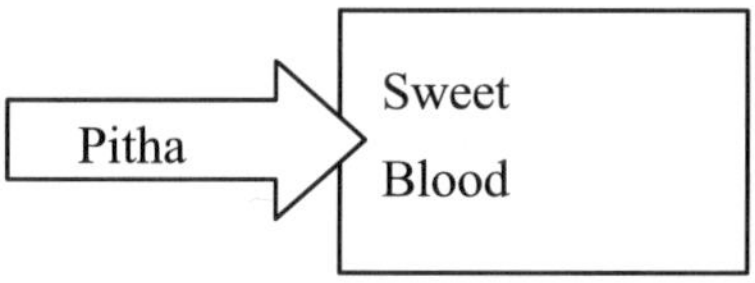

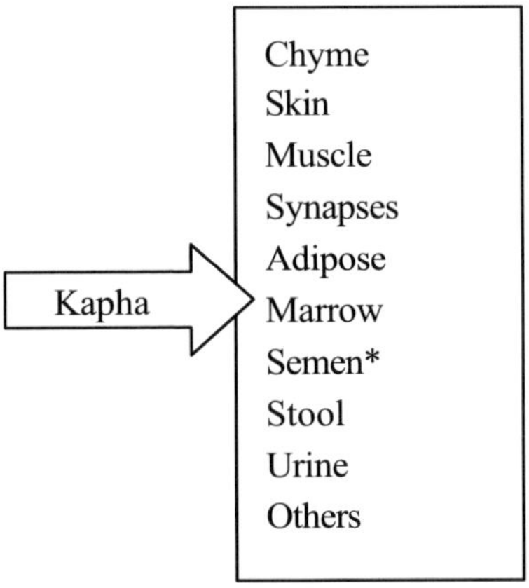

Due to the interdependency between *dosha, dhaatu* and *mala*, the 'condition (s)' that acts on one of them also affects others. For instance, *the condition, the substance, or the medicine* that increases *pitha* will make a quantitative and qualitative increase on sweat, blood and vice versa.

This forms a treatment law.

In *vridhi* (increment) and *kshaya* (decrement) both quantitative and qualitative aspects are considered.

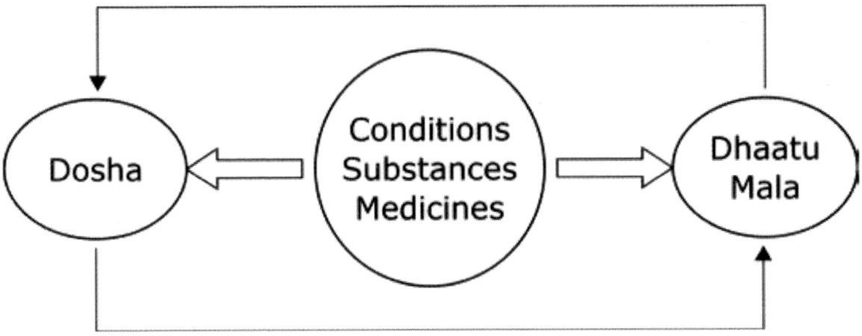

VATA dosha has exception from this law.

BRIMHANA and LANGHANA

Brimhana (Addition) is a treatment procedure for *Dhaatu Pushti* (Nourishment) where *Kapha* increases and *Vata* decreases. *Kapha* is constructive and *Vata* destructive in nature. In other sense, there is no *brimhana* (nourishment) without *Kapha* increase. On the contrary, in *Langhana* (Abstinence)), *Kapha* decreases and *Vata* increases. It is a destructive process. The effect of *Langhana* is trimming and it cannot be achieved without *Vata* increase. So the treatment principles are opposite. To increase Vata, the treatment option is a curtailment procedure.

The effect of *Brimhana* on Vata and Kapha

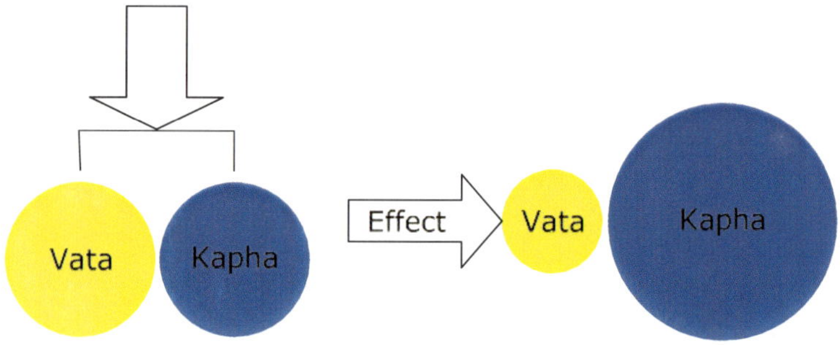

The terms *Vridhi* (increment) and *Kshaya* (decrement) represents vitiation.

Brimhana and *Langhana* are two treatment procedures in Ayurveda. The action brought about by *Brimhana* (the augmentation technic for nutritional and immunological factors) is *Vridhi*; and by *Langhana* (abating of Pathological factors) is *Kshaya*. This may confuse with the same terminologies (*Vridhi* and *Kshaya*) used in the vitiation, where it represents the disruption of homeostasis.

The effect of *Langhana*

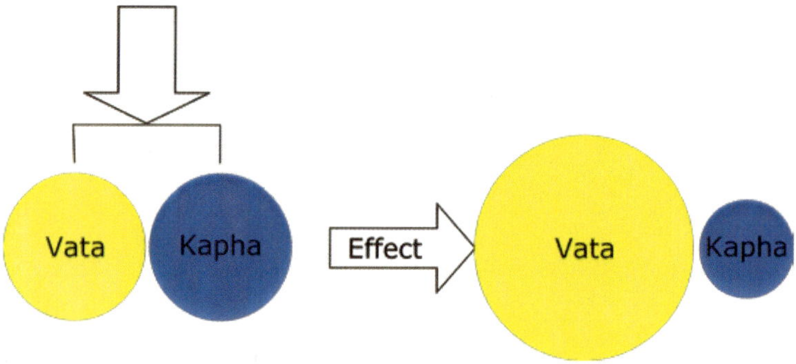

The aim of a treatment with *Langhana* is 'to decrease' the pathological factors that disrupt the homeostasis.

Brimhana is a repairing technique

Langhana is an approach against the cause and symptoms of the disease.

OJUS (THE NATURAL IMMUNITY)

Ojus is the 'lustre' or the essence of the *Saptha dhaatu* (table 11). It is the principle of vitality in the body, providing both heat and action, including the virility and the generative power. The ultimate refined result of di gestion, absorption and assimilation, 'the Ojus' is a wholesome biochemical substance that nourishes all the body tissues and directly influences the nature and quality of physical, mental and emotional life. Its primary location is heart from which it circulates to all parts of the body.

It is 'the deha-bala' (the power of defense) against the attack of potential diseases. The Ojus-deficient body is susceptible to all sorts of diseases.

The comparison of 'Ojus' with modern immunology is a risk since its history is slightly more than 100 years, if we consider Louis Pasteur as the "Father of immunology" as most do. Present immunology is more precise than what Ayurvedic views have about *Ojus or 'dehabala'* which infact refers to '*the innate power in body to defend disease or to keep a s tate of homeostasis*. Agnivesha samhitha, the authentic Ayurvedic reference to the later *Acharyas* is in 600 BC. The Charaka Samhita is believed to be a re-work of Agnivesha samhitha, dated back to 1 AD.

The real history of cellular immunology begins in the late 1950's. The natural immunity whether according to classical Ayurvedic understanding or t he latest, acting as the first line of defense, rapid in action, and not very discriminating in what it attacks is highly effective in keeping us free of infection most of the time. The immune system includes all of the *structures* and *processes* that provide against potential *pathogens*. The *structures* in this reference constitute '*Saptha dhaatu*'; the '*processes*', their proper transition untill the end dhaatu - *Shukra.* Ayurveda as a healing system advocates a perfect life style, with the main aim of keeping the immunity intact.

Ojus is described, as reddish yellow oily, located in the heart and distributed throughout the body; but not defined as a gross structure. It is responsible for the higher states of consciousness, purity of thoughts, perfect health, positive feelings, love, joy, better immunity, longevity, intelligence, creativity, memory, bliss and thought process. The aim of prophylaxis in Ayurveda is to amplify the ojus which in turn boosts the immunity.

The body's defence mechanism to protect itself may be

Specific or Non-specific.

Non-specific mechanisms are two types

First line of defence: where a mechanical barrier such as skin or mucous membrane blocks the entry of bacteria or harmful substance to the tissues. Associated with these mechanical barriers are body secretions such as saliva or tears that contain enzymes or chemicals that destroy foreign materials.

The Second line of defence: includes the nonspecific processes of phagocytosis and inflammation. Phagocytosis is the processes by which the neutrophils and macrophages randomly engulf and destroy the bacteria, cell debris, or foreign matter. Interferons are nonspecific agents that protect against virus.

Specific defense mechanism is the third line of defence mechanism. It provides protection by stimulating a unique response following exposure to specific foreign substances. It is similar to a surveillance system, warning of attack and subsequent mobilization of an army for defence! Because of unique antigen (often a protein) on the surface of an individual's cells, that person's immune system can distinguish *self* from *non-self* (foreign) and can thus detect and destroy unknown material. Normally immune system ignores "self" cells, but recognizes a specific invader antigen as foreign and develops specific response to that particular antigen and stores that particular response in its memory cells for future reference if the invader returns.

CHAPTER –4

Etiological factors of Ayurveda

THE CAUSE

That which gives rise to an action is called 'cause'. In medical science we need to find and justify a cause. Let us see the Ayurvedic hypothetical perspective of cause.

As to cause and effect, cause precedes the effect, but that, in order to be a true cause, it must be a constant antecedent, and the effect must be unconditionally subsequent to it. There is an important and often neglected difference between *Karana* (instrumental) and *Kaarana* (the cause). The former, though it may mean cause, is properly the instrumental cause only, or simply the instrument. An axe, for instance, is the *Karana*, or instrument, in felling a tree, but it is not the *Kaarana*, or the real cause.

Causes are threefold:

(1) Intimate (2) Non-intimate (3) Instrumental

The threads, for instance, are the intimate cause of the cloth, the sewing of the threads the non-intimate, and the shuttle the instrumental cause.

Cause and effect are seen as different temporal aspects of the same thing - the effect lies latent in the cause which in turn seeds the next effect.

Here we are concerned about Ayurvedic view of the pathological cause. Under this heading we will discuss (1) Seasons (2) Food (3) Activities (4) Sense organs and (5) Deformed dhaatu.

1. The Seasons (*Ritu*) and Tridosha

The Indian climate has a cycle of six seasons. There are areas where the distinction of the seasons is felt, but in most areas the six seasons overlap. They are:

1. Greeshma (Summer) -- May to June

2. Varsha (Monsoon) -- July to September

3. Sharat (Autumn) -- September to Mid November

4. Hemanta (Pre winter) -- Mid November to Mid December

5. Sishira (Winter) -- Mid December to Mid February

6. Vasanta (Spring) -- Mid February to April

Seasonal influence result in two types of dosha vitiation

a) *Chaya*: The increment of dosha at its own site is called as 'Chaya'. Refer to the different locations of dosha (Table 8, 9 and 10). The symptoms of 'Chaya' is inferred from the detectable disgust in patient to the cause of 'chaya' and likeness to the opposite factors.

b) *Prakopa*: This is the migration of dosha through or to other sites quitting abode.

Restlessness and onset of disease are the signs of 'prakopa'. (Prakopa is combination of two words. 'Kopa' in Sanskrit denotes 'an increase or accumulation; prakopa is state of more accumulation)

Ayurvedic definition of perfect health

Samadosha samadhaatu samagnischa malakriya
Prasannatmendriya: mana:

Swasta ityabhidheeyate (S.S)

Perfect health is a condition with (1) Normal dosha, dhaatu, and digestive enzymes (2) Normal excretory functions and (3) Normal soul, sense organs and mind.

This represents a condition with normal physiology, metabolism, excretory function, sense organs, nervous system and state of mind.

Life has proven to be far more complexthan human imagination could have conceived.

Cells are not bags of Tridosha and Panchamahabhoota as envisoned over centuries ago; but rather structurally complexand dynamic

Multicellular organisms, consists of several hundred cell types, must coordinate a huge number of biochemical processes. A stable environment, called *homeostasis,* is maintained by the dynamic interplay between opposing processes. Perfect health occurs in such a condition.

The mechanism of *Chaya, Prakopa* and *Prashamana* (normalisation) of Dosha

The Principle of Ayurvedic treatment is based on two views: (1) *Like factors cause an increase (2) Unlike factors cause a decrease.* This can be compared to the terms like synergism or additivism and antagonism.

Vata dosha and seasons

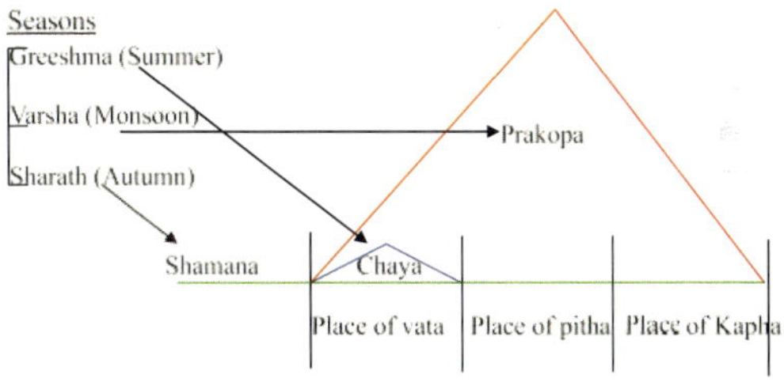

How Vata is vitiated to chaya during GREESHMA (Summer) and to prakopa during VARSHA (Monsoon)

During summer as sun and wind are extremely potent (theekshna) hot (ushna) and dry (rooksha), the vegetations, animals on the earth and our body turn rooksha (dry) and laghu (light) which are identical to the features of Vata dosha. In fact this situations should make vata get in to a kopa stage. Since the quality of the season is hot which is opposite character of vata (Sheetha - cold) there is no chance of vata gets in to 'kopa' stage during summer; only 'chaya' occurs. But during Varsha (Monsoon) due to the coldness of the sea- son, which is identical to vata character, it is vitiated to kopa stage. The cold- ness is most sensible character of the Vata. Many Vata diseases increase in the cold climate.

Characteristic features of Vata	Opposite features of Vata
Rooksha (Dryness)	Snigdha (Oily)
Laghu (Light)	Guru (Heavy)
Sheetha (Cold)	**Ushna (Hot)**
Ghara (Solid)	Slashna (Viscous)
Sookshma (Micro)	Sthoola (Macro)
Chala (Moving)	Sthira (Hardened)

Table. 18 Features of Vata

1. Characteristic features of Vata + Ushna (Hot) of Summer result in Chaya of Vata

2. Characteristic features of Vata + Sheetha (Cold) of Monsoon result in Kopa.

3. Opposite features of Vata + Ushna (Hot) of Autumn result in Shamana

(Common in Autumn)

Pitha dosha and seasons

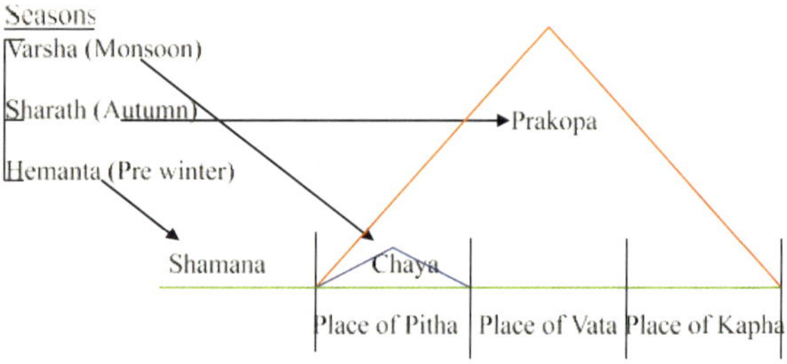

How Pitha is vitiated to chaya during VARSHA (Monsoon) and to prakopa during SHARATH (Autumn)

The rain on the hot earth during the monsoon brings out steamy vapor from the surface, which makes the water and vegetation acidic (Amla paka). Consumption of this makes pitha vitiate to chaya. The coldness of this season, which is the opposite feature of Pitha prevents it from vitiated to kopa. But during Sharath since there is prominent presence of sun, the heat vitiates the pitha to Kopa.

Characteristic features of Pitha		Opposite features of Pitha	
Sneha	(Fatty)	Rooksha	(Dry)
Theekshna	(Potent)	Manda	(Sluggish)
Ushna	**(Hot)**	**Sheetha**	**(Cold)**
Laghu	(Light)	Guru	(Heavy)
Visram	(Purulent)	Vishada	(Clear)
Saram	(Spreading)	Sthira	(Stationary)
Dravam	(Liquid)	Sandra	(Solid)

Table. 19 Features of Pitha

1. Characteristic features of Pitha + Sheetha (Cold) of Monsoon result in Chaya of Pitha
2. Characteristic features of Pitha + Ushna (Hot)) of Autumn result in Kopa.
3. Opposite features of Pitha + Sheetha (Cold) of Pre Winter result in Shamana (Common in Pre winter)

Kapha dosha and seasons

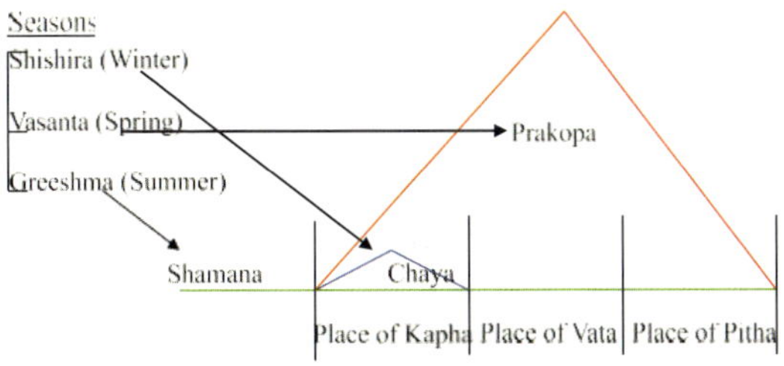

How Kapha is vitiated to chaya during SHISHIRA (Winter) and to prakopa during VASANTA (Spring)?

During winter the water, vegetations and body achieve the identical features of Kapha, the Snigdha (oily) Sheetha (cold) Guru (heavy) etc. These qualities vitiate kapha to chaya. The identical condition of the season, food and body make kapha dosha to become solid (khannathwa) and prevents it dislocate from abode to cause Kopa.

We have seen that Kopa is the increase of doshas with a migration through and to other dosha sites. In spring due to heat of the sun the solidified Kapha loosens and it is vitiated to kopa.

Characteristic features of Kapha		Opposite features of Kapha	
Snigdha	(Oily	Rooksha	(Dry)
Sheetha	**(Cold)**	**Ushna**	**(Hot)**
Guru	(Heavy)	Laghu	(Light)
Manda	(Sluggish)	Theekshna	(Potent)
Slashna	(Viscous)	Parusha	(Rough)
Mritsna	(Pasty)	Vishada	(Clear)
Sthira	(Stationary)	Chala	(Moving)

Table. 20 Features of Kapha

1. Characteristic features of Kapha + Sheetha (Cold) of Winter result in Chaya of Pitha
2. Characteristic features of Kapha + Ushna (Hot) of Spring result in Kopa.
3. Opposite features of Kapha + Ushna (Hot) of Summer result in Shamana

Different varieties of di seases occur during Varsha (Monsoon seasons). Besides cold and influenza, many diseases exacerbate during winter. A change of immune response may be set up in this seasons due to the fluctuating temperature. There is Ayurvedic explanation for this phenomenon. Look at the above changes in tridosha during different seasons, as simplified in the following table:

Dosha	Greeshma	Varsha	Sharath	Hemanta	Shishira	Vasanta
Vata	Chaya	Kopa	Shamana			
Pitha		Chaya	Kopa	Shamana		
Kapha	Shamana				Chaya	Kopa

Table. 21 Stages of dosha vitiation on season (rithu)

During Varsha (Monsoon) both Vata and Pitha are etiolological, former in Kopa and later in Chaya. Due to these conditions diseases occur more in Varsha. Note that in none of ot her season dual dosha vitiated etiological stage occurs.

We learned that vitiation of dosha is influenced by the climatic features like hot (ushna) and cold (sheetha). Raining or pouring (Varsha) is also a characteristic feature of a season.

So let us consider the seasonal habits as following:

1. Hot (ushna) in summer
2. Cold (sheetha) in winter
3. Pouring (varsha) in monsoon.

Season's manifestation in 'proper time and adequate habits' has great influence on the stability of tridosha. Unnatural occurance of seasons contribute to the factors of dosha vitiation.

Seasonal features	Hypo (heena)	Hyper (Athi)	Unnatural (mithya)
Hot	Less or nil during respective season	Excessive during respective season	Occur during other season
Cold	Less or nil during respective season	Excessive during respective season	Occur during other season
Rain	Less or nil during respective season	Excessive during respective season	Occur during other Season

Table 22 Unnatural status of the seasons

2. **Food and Tridosha**

Food also vitiate tridosha to chaya and kopa having qualities capable of causing it. For this reason specific food and combinations are advised to balance tridosha. Substances consumed as food are categorized with the properties of tridosha.

Sanskrit name	Botanical/Zoological & (English name)	Product	Action of tridosha
Rakta Sali	Oriza Sativa (Rice)	Whole grain rice without removing bran layer and germ	Tridosha hara (Pacify tridosha)
Yava	Hordeum vulgare (Barley)	Grain of barley	Increases kapha and pitha
Godhuma	Triticum aestuvum (Wheat)	Grain of wheat	Pacify vata and pitha
Shimbija	Fabaceae family (Legumes)	Pulses	Increases pitha and kapha
Gomamsa	Bos indicus (Cattle)	Meat	Vata pacifying
Ajamamsa	Copra aegagrus (Goat)	Meat	Do not vitiate any dosha as its flesh is similar to human flesh, according to Ayurveda
Matsya	(Fish)	Fish	Most of the fishes increases pitha and kapha but pacify Vata

Table. 23 Few examples showing the influence of food on tridosha.

3. **Activities and Tridosha**

Physical (Deha), Verbal (Vak) and Mental (Chitha) distorted activities also can become the factors for dosha vitiation. This happens in three ways, hypo, hyper and unnatural (heena yoga, athiyoga and mithyayoga

Activities	Hypo (heena)	Hyper (athi)	Unnatural (mithya)
Physical	Hypopraxia (Abnormally Diminished Activity)	Hyperpraxia (Excessive activity, Restlessness)	Holding and forcing the excretory process, extraordinary physical activates
Verbal	Voice holding	Voice strain	Speaking during Deglutition
Mental	Hyponoia (dulled(mental	Tension	Doing sin

Table. 24 Unnatural activities

4. **Sense organs and tridosha**

Five sense organs - skin, eyes, nostrils, ears and tongue perform their normal functions on contact with their respective objectives. Their hypo, hyper and unnatural association with the objects (*indriyartha*) cause dosha vitiation capable of developing diseases.

Sense organs	Hypo (heena)	Hyper (athi)	Unnatural
Skin	Abstinence from light	Over exposure to heat/cold/ humidity	Contact with high roughness, chemicals etc.
Eye	Viewing in dim light	Viewing brighter sparks	Viewing micro/ macro objects; viewing solar eclipse with naked eyes
Nostrils	Strained olfaction like smelling the lightest smells	Over exposure to normal smells	Smelling strongly pungent/allergents
Ears	Listening to micro decibels (strained hearing)	Over exposure to normal hearing	Listening to high decibel sounds
Tongue	Improper tasting	Over tasting, hyper phagia	Tasting corrosives/Poisons

Table.25 Unnatural activities of sense organs

5. **Deformed Dhaatu**

Stability of *saptha dhaatu*, both structural and functional, in genesis, transition and final build up is significant in normal health. The specific energy needed for each *dhaatu* to form, nourish, function, and transform to the next is called *dhaatwagni*. Its defect cause imperfect genesis of the follower. This may be primitive explanation of 'growth'. The factors controlling growth is called 'growth factors'. Its deficiency causes imperfect genesis. Dhaatwagni, responsible for the development of dhaatu may be compared to *growth factors*. Defects in these factors can cause excessive growth (eg. Tumours) or disintegration (eg. Lysis or degenerative changes).

Each dhaatu is developed from a previous one by specific *Agni*.

Dhaatwagni	**Dhaatu-Formed**	**Role of each *Agni***		
		Sanskrit terms	**English terms**	**Scientific**
Jadaragni*	Rasa	Rasa vardhana	Formation of chyme	Chymopoiesis
Rasa dhaatwagni	Rakta	Rakta vardhana	Formation of blood	Hemopoiesis
Rakta dhaatwagni	Mamsa	Mamsa vardhana	Formation of muscles	Myogenesis
Mamṣa dhaatwagni	Medha	Medho vardhana	Formation of fat	Lipogenesis
Medḥa dhaatwagni	Asthi	Asthi vardhana	Formation of bone	Osteogenesis
Asthi dhaatwagni	Majja	Majja vardhana	Formation of marrow	Bone marrow formation
Majja dhaatwagni	Shukra	Shukra vardhana	Formation of sperm/ovum	Spermatogenesis/

Table. 26 Dhaatwagni and their role (*Jadaragni is digestive enzymes)

A state of health is difficult to define because the genetic differences among individuals as well as the many variations in life experiences and environmental influences create a variable base. The context in which health is measured is also a consideration.

Disease develop when significant changes occur in the body, leading to a state in which homeostasis cannot be maintained. In this condition relatively constant or stable internal environment is maintained within the body with regard to all the vital body functions. As frequent minor changes occur in the body, the compensation mechanisms respond, and the homeostasis is quickly restored. Usually the individual is not aware of these changes or the compensations taking place. Infact, *tridosha-panchamahabuta knowledge* is not simply sufficient to explain health and disease though Ayurveda is voluminously theorized and dogmatized with those philosophies.

CHAPTER 5

Pharmacodynamics of Ayurveda

What the drug does to the body is Pharmacodynamics and what the body does to the drug is Pharmacokinetics. The former deals with the physiological and biochemical effects of the drugs and their mechanism of action at macromolecular, subcellular and organ system levels; the later refers to movements of the drug in and alteration of the drug by the body which includes absorption, distribution, binding, localization, storage, biotransformation and excretion of the drug.

Orthodox philosophy is a part and parcel of Ayurveda. Even now Pharmacodynamics and Pharmacokinetics of Ayurveda are taught philosophically! Let us go to such fundamentals.

Panchamahabhoota, the five physical elements according to Ayurveda is the basis of all cosmic creation. They are *tanmatra,* meaning rudimentary, subtle or mere essence. According to Ayurveda philosophy there are two primordial cosmic principles; the *Purusha* and *Prakriti.*

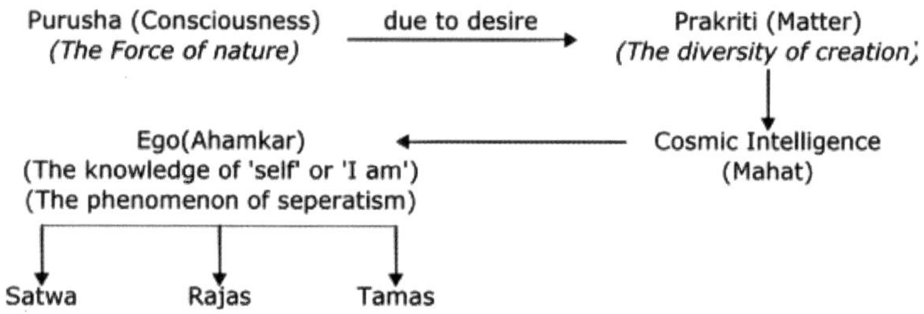

Purusha and Prakrithi are eternal principles, the reason behind existence of life; former is the male aspect and later the female aspect of creation. 'Prakrithi' is the principle of desire from which 'a cosmic intelligence' referred to as *Mahat* took origin. From Mahat, Ego (*Ahamkar*), the knowledge of 'self' or 'I am' originated. This phenomenon is a kind of separatism or individualization, each of us is having! '*Ahamkar*' (ego) manifests the three qualities, Satwa, Rajas and Tamas.

Satwa	Rajas	Tamas
Virtue, Beautiful, good, wise Intelligence, self consciousness	Passion Active, fierce, Energy	Dullness Dark, stupid, ugly, Sloth

Table 27. The basic components of creation

- Satwa is creative potential
- Rajas the kinetic protective force and
- Tamas is the potential destructive force.

Tanmatra

'Tanmatra' concept arises from *Tamas*. Five tanmatra, the sub atomic aspects of the material universe perceived by the five 'njanedriya' (Sense organs) are formed from the *Tamas*. They are:

1. Shabda (Sound)
2. Sparsa (Touch)
3. Roopa (Sight)
4. Rasa (Taste)
5. Gandha (Smell)

From each of these the basic principle of universe, the primary components of all matter called 'Panchamahaboota' take origin. 'Pancha' means 'five', and 'mahabhoota' means the 'minutest ever possible element', unidentifiably minute!

Sanskrit name	English meaning	The Concept
Prithwi	Earth	Solid
Ap	Water	Liquid
Thej	Fire	Energy
Vayu	Air	Gas
Akash	Ether	Space

Table. 28 Panchamahabhoota

The five elements form the constituents of matter and account for different faculties of human experience. They are also associated with overall health of human being organised by the energy, structure, function, and the phenomenon of life! This link between the material universe and the living body is the key to the pharmacodynamics of Ayurveda. '*Nothing on the earth is non medicinal'*. The disrupted homeostasis in *Panchamahabhootatmaka shareera* (the body made of the five elements) can be corrected with *Panchamahabhootatmaka dravya* (the substances made of the same five elements.) This supports the statement that everything on the earth is medicinal, if properly chosen and used.

How Ayurvedic drugs work?

A physician should be aware of the movements of drugs within biological system as affected by uptake, distribution, elimination and biotransformation to explain the action of a therapeutic drug. Let us see how we can relate such actions to the hypothetical explanations in Ayurveda. Accordingly the drugs act in the body due to the following (therapeutic) properties.

1. Rasa (Taste)
2. Guna (Quality)
3. Veerya (Potency)
4. Vipaka (The bio transformation)
5. Prabhava (Influence)

RASA (The taste as therapeutic agent)

The sensation produced by a suitable stimulus applied to the gustatory nerve endings in the tongue is called as the taste (Rasa). This is identified by the chemoreceptors on t he tongue called as the gustatory (taste) receptors. Chemosensory stimulation triggers a cascade of molecular and cellular events that are translated into a signal for the nervous system. The encoded information is then transmitted to the appropriate brain areas to initiate and maintain the sensory response.

In Western medicine most drugs are coated and masked to neutralize their taste and smell. Ayurveda, however consider the taste (*rasa*) as one of the fundamental active principles of therapeutics. Tastes can stimulate or turn off digestive processes, and determine the components of di gestion to form a (Ayurvedic) therapeutic agent. Different tastes combine in various ways and are influenced by the sense of smell, thus permitting a wide variety of different sensory experiences. Ayurveda explains six types of tastes - *Swad, Amla, Lavana, Thiktha, Ushna, and Kashaya.*

Ayurvedic Terminology	**English terminology**	**Western medicine**
1.Swad	Sweet	1. Sweet
2.Lavana	Salt	2. Salty
3.Thiktha	Bitter	3. Bitter
4.Amla	Sour	4.Sour
5.Kashaya	Astrigent	
6.Ushna	Pungent	

Table. 29 The tastes

Sensory Mechanisms of Rasa.

Scientific and Ayurvedic concepts of taste

a) **Modern concept:** Sweet, Salty, Bitter and Sour tastes are felt by the following mechanisms. Recently a fifth taste was introduced in the Western medicine, with the help of the food industry, called *Umami* which describes the taste of certain Amino acids (Glutamate, Aspartate, and related compounds).

1. **Sweet:** A sweet taste is sensed by receptors in the apical membrane that binds glucose and other carbohydrates. The receptors then activate gustducin and cAMP production by adenylate cyclase. The elevated levels of cAMP cause PKA -mediated phosphorylation of K^{+} channels, which inhibits the receptors. Depolarization occurs, followed by Ca^{2+} entry through the depolarized channels; transmitters are then released, which results in increased firing in the primary afferent nerve. (PKA - Protein Kinase A is a family of enzymes)

2. **Sour:** A sour taste is the result of increased proton concentration H^{+} (higher than in the water). H^{+} ions block K^{+} channels that are responsible for maintaining proper hyperpolarized membrane potential (-85 mV). Blocking these channels causes depolarization and Ca^{2+} dependent transmitter release that results in increased firing of the primary afferent nerve.

3. **Salty:** A salty taste is triggered by ions such as sodium chloride entering the cells via the appropriate ion channels, in this case Na^{+}- channel. The entry of Na^{+} causes depolarization; transmitter release occurs and results in stimulation of the primary afferent nerve.

4. **Bitter:** A bitter taste is mediated via IP_3 second messenger action, and Ca^{2+} is released from internal stores. The elevated Ca^{2+} then triggers transmitter release and firing in the primary afferent nerve. (Inositol triphosphate3 (IP3) is important second messenger)

b) **Ayurvedic concept:** A taste is sensed due to *Panchamahabutha* components of *dravya* (matter); and difference in taste is due to the variety combination of *panchamahabhoota.*

Rasa	Panchamahabhoota combination
1 Swad (Sweet)	Prithwi (Earth) + Ap (Water)
2 Amla (Sour)	Prithwi (Earth) + Agni (Fire)
3 Lavana (Salty)	Ap (Water) + Agni (Fire)
4 Thiktha (Bitter)	Vayu (Air) + Akash (Ether)
5 Ushna (Pungent)	Agni (Fire) + Vayu (Air)
6 Kashaya (Astringent)	Prithwi (Earth) + Vayu (Air)

Table. 30 Panchamahabhoota constitution of rasa

According to Ayurveda a medicine's curative effect is due to *panchamahabhoota* constitution of the active rasa of the drug. Constitution of the patient (*prakrithi*) and the status of tridosha also matters.

Remember that '*dosha vitiation*' is the immediate cause of all diseases. Tridosha also have a panchamahabhuta structure. *Ap* (Water) and *Pritwi* (Earth) are the constituents of *Kapha dosha*. *Akash* (Ether) and *Vayu* (Air) that of *Vata*. *Teja* (Agni) alone forms *Pita*.

Combination of Panchamahabhoota	Constituted dosha
	Kapha 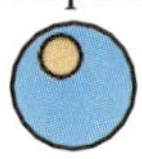
	Pita 
	Vata 

Table. 31 Panchamahabhutha constitution of tridosha

Colours are assigned for illustration only

Prithwi (Earth) Ap

(Water)

Agni (Fire) Vayu

(Air)

Akash (Ether)

Tridosha – the energy of living body

Some critics do not accept 'the energy concept of Tridosha'. Tridosha are invisible; it is a 'hypothetical tool' to explain physiological function of the body. Let us consider it as the energy to perform the functions in the *panchamahabhootata constituted* body.

All *life processes* consists of chemical reactions catalyzed by enzymes. The reactions in a living organism, which are known collectively as metabolism result in highly coordinated and purposeful activity. Conceptually tridosha control only the living body. Panchamahabhoota elements constitute structure of the body (even if not alive). Tridosha, *'either the catalyzed enzymes or the energy'* give *life processes* to such a constitution. *Shadrasa* (six tastes) could be acting as catalyst or inhibitor in the process.

Rasa	Shamana (inhibitor) of	Vardhana (Stimulant) of
Swad (Sweet) Amla (Sour Lavana (Salty)	Vata	Kapha
Thiktha (Bitter) Ushna (Pungent) Kashaya (Astringent)	Kapha	Vata
Kashaya (Astringent) Thiktha (Bitter) Swad (Sweet)	Pitha	
Amla (Sour) Lavana (Salty) Ushna (Pungent)		Pitha

Table. 32 Action of shadrasa on tridosha

Ayurveda do not know microbiology. Therefore, a concept of a microbiocidal or microbiostatic agent is not in place. Aim of Ayurvedic treatment is updating tridosha, either a top up or a cut down to build up homeostasis; or *anabolic* (Brimhana) or *catabolic* (Langhana) approach.

Vata is catabolic and Kapha is anabolic. Pitha being the *Agni* (fire) element can either be catabolic or anabolic. Any substance, food or drug causing **Vata inhibition** will aid constructive metabolism (**Anabolism**) and those causing the **Kapha inhibition** will aid destructive metabolism (**Catabolism**). In table 29 we saw that Swad (sweet), Amla (sour), and Lanava (salty) are Vata shamana (**Vatagna**) – **ANTI CATABOLIC**. But they stimulate Kapha (**Sleshmala**) – **ANABOLIC**. Anti catabolic and anabolic properties of these rasas together may make them strongly anabolic.

Likewise Thiktha (bitter), Ushna (Pungent) and Kashaya (Astringent) are capable of inhibiting Kapha (**Kaphagna**) –**ANTI ANABOLIC**. They also stimulate or make Vata (**Vataja**) –**CATABOLIC**. Anti anabolic and catabolic properties of these rasas together may make them strongly catabolic.

Kashaya (Astringent) Thiktha (Bitter) and Swad (sweet), are the pitha inhibitors (**Pithagna**)-**ANTI ANABOLIC**) or (**PRO CATABOLIC**). Amla (Sour), Lavana (Salty) and Ushna (Pungent) rasas are pitha stimulators (**Paithika**) – (**PRO ANABOLIC**)

Rasa	Shamana (reduce/ inhibit)	Vardhana (increase/ stimula
Swad (Sweet)	Vata & Pitha Energy	Kapha energy
Amla (Sour)	Vata energy	Kapha & Pitha energy
Lavana (Salty)	Vata energy	Kapha & Pitha energy
Thiktha (Bitter)	Pitha & Kapha energy	Vata energy
Ushna (Pungent)	Kapha energy	Vata & Pitha energy
Kashaya (Astringent)	Pitha & Kapha energy	Vata energy

Table. 33 Catalystic action of each rasa on tridosha

The summerised therapeutic effects of rasa (comparable to metabolism)

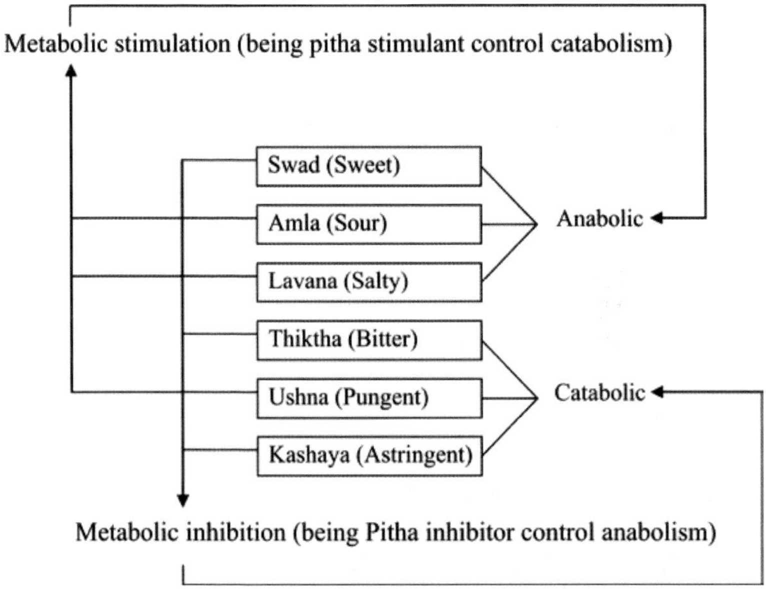

GUNA (the therapeutic quality of matter)

Ayurveda consider ten opposite pairs of qualities of the matter for the therapeutic purpose. These qualities may be representing synergestic and antagonistic actions with the like and unlike properties respectively (*Vrudhi: samane: sarvesham; Vipareethe viparyaya*)".

No	Quality	No	Opposite quality
1	Guru (Heavy/macromolecular)	2	Laghu (Light/micromolecular)
3	Manda (Sluggish/slow acting)	4	Theekshna (Potent)
5	Hima (Cold/endergonic)	6	Ushna (Hot/exergonic)
7	Snigdha (Oily)	8	Rooksha (Dry/unhydrous)
9	Slakshna (Viscous/glutinous)	10	Khara (Solid/without interstices)
11	Sandra (Colloid)	12	Drava (Liquid/more watery)
13	Mridu (Soft)	14	Kadina (Hard)
15	Sthira (Stable)	16	Chala (Unstable)
17	Sookshma (Minute)	18	Sthoola (Large)
19	Vishada (Clear)	20	Pichila (Cloudy)

Table. 34 Properties of matter (dravya)

Guru and Laghu

The property 'guru' refers to that which is not easily digestible. A molecule of colloidal size notably proteins and polysaccharides can be considered as having this quality. Ayurveda takes much importance on gastro intestinal system and digestive processes in considering any disease and its treatment. Gastro intestinal tract (Koshta) is considered as the seat of all diseases. 'Laghu' means easily digestible materials. The stomach has little effort to digest this kind of food or drug, easily converting into materials suitable for assimilation, synthesis of tissues or liberation of energy.

Manda and Theekshna

'Manda' (slow acting) and 'Theekshna' (potent) explain therapeutic potency. Some medicines are slow acting (manda) by generation. Long acting (LA) compounds or time releasing (TR) compounds also comes under the definition of this property. 'Theekshna' (potent) exhibits an immediate action. Toxins and corrosives come under this group. Ayurveda have natural detoxification procedures (Sudhi) of such substances for safe therapeutic consumption.

Hima and Ushna

Hima or Sheetha (cool) and Ushna (hot) properties of drugs according to Ayurveda are not simple physical properties, therapeutically these two qualities of drugs can rather be considered as a 'conversive' aspect. The paradoxical statement that this drug is hot and that one is cold is something very vague. The conversive heat or cool effect is the hot or cold produced in the body by the absorption of waves which are not hot or cold themselves. I prefer this explanation because substances having explained to have Ushna (hot) or Sheetha/Hima (cool) effect in the body are not as such physically hot or cool. Based on their therapeutic activity they are categorized like this. Most of such drugs are stimulators or catalysts of digestion and metabolism (Pitha stimulators) when they are branded Ushna (hot) and suppressers or inhibitors or even antagonists (Pitha inhibitors) when Hima (cool). By the view of chemistry of such materials it could be also the concept of exergonic and endergonic properties. Therefore, Sheetha and Ushna represent the efficacy of a drug/food.

Snigdha and Rooksha

'Snigdha' refers to an unctuous feel. Oils and creams are of this type. Snigdha is the characteristic feature of fats and oils. Externally this quality nourishes oily structure of skin. Internally it is pitha inhibitory. The digestive enzymes are pitha in nature. The modern science had proved that the presence of fat in chyme stimulates duodenum to secret hormone enterogastrone that inhibits gastric secretion. This is because of the chemistry of fat and refers to 'this dravya quality' mentioned in Ayurveda as snigdha. Thus, simple mentioning of a pharmaceutical quality as 'snigdha' (oily) has a deep reference.

'Rooksha' means dry or unhydrous. Though mentioned as the opposite of 'snigdha' it is not merely lack of oily but also that of moisture. The external feel or look of dryness gives an idea of this quality. Presence of water has great significance in the chemical structure of a substance.

Slakshna and Khara

Viscosity, 'slakshna' in general is the resistance to flow or alteration of shape, by any substance as a result of molecular cohesion; a term most frequently applied to liquids. Water has a low viscosity and glycerol has high. 'Khara', the solid is without interstices and cavities and non cancellous. This structural identification in therapeutic point of view is significant in Ayurveda with different spectrum of activities both physical and chemical.

Sandra and Drava

'Sandra', the colloid, is aggregation of atoms of molecules in a finely divided sub microscopic state, dispersed in gaseous, liquid, or solid medium and resisting sedimentation, diffusion and filtration, thus differing from precipitation. But the liquid state mentioned as 'Drava' is with different bonding, free flowing and the solvent to the solutes.

Mridu and Kadina

'Mridu' (Soft) and 'Kadina' (Hard) are the external feel of substances. Compare softness of cotton with hardness of coral when both are considered for certain kinds of physical treatment purposes.

Sthira and Chala

'Sthira', the stability and 'Chala', the un-stability of substances are the reactive changes in the morphology of dravya (drugs) due to the influence of external environment or when in contact with other substances, rather than the state of being stationary or moving respectively, which have little pharmacological importance.

Sookshma and Sthoola

'Sookshma' represents the minute and 'Sthoola' the large structure of substances used as drugs. With present knowledge minute can go up to 'micro'. When prefixed to a term denoting a unit of any kind, it is one-millionth of such unit. Ayurveda mention 'Paramanu (Sub-atomic) concept' in its philosophy.

Vishada and Pichila

'Vishada' (Clear) and 'Pichila' (Cloudy) represent features of liquids representing purity and impurity respectively. Clear water or uncontaminated fluids are said to be 'vishada' (pure). Contaminated fluid or pus is 'Pichila' (cloudy) in nature.

Out of twenty properties of substances (drugs) we examined, only the first six (Guru, Laghu, Manda, Theekshna, Hima/Sheetha and Ushna) are valuable in Ayurvedic pharmacodynamics while others are rather morphologically important. These qualities are to a greater extent helpful in pharmacognosy.

VEERYA (The Potency)

The pharmacological activity of a drug/compound is known as potency. It is the force or strength by which the drug acts. This is a quantitative property and is measurable. In Ayurveda, the *veerya* is represented as Ushna (hot) and Sheetha (cool). Similar terms are also used among the properties of matter which we discussed above. Here they represent the active potencies in a therapeutic action. The concept of potency and efficacy are often confused and interchangeably used within the scientific and pharmaceutical industry.

Ushna veerya can be a source (of power) enabling to do work under suitable conditions. Eg. Digestive, mucolytics, thrombolytics etc. It could be also synergetics, catalysts and stimulants. Sheetha veerya is not merely the opposite but similar source (of force) to perform a therapeutic activity. Eg. Antipyretic, Anti inflammatory, Anti depressant etc. It may also be the antagonists, blockades and inhibitor. With modern techniques potency of a drug can be evaluated and fixed as required for the desired therapeutic effect according to age, body weight and disease conditions.

In Ayurveda food, single drugs and drug combinations are categorized as Ushna veerya (hot) and Sheetha veerya (cool).

VIPAKA (Pharmacologically active drug metabolite)

Vipaka refers to the biotransformed stage of food or medicine in the gastro intestinal tract after digestion. It is the therapeutically active metabolite of the drug. According to Ayurveda it is the change of rasa (the taste) of dravyam (food/drug) after digestion. Six tastes are transformed to **three Vipaka.**

Rasa	Vipaka
1. Madhura (Sweet) 2. Lavana (Salty)	1. Madhura (Sweet)
3. Amla (Sour)	2. Amla (Sour/acidic)
4. Katu/Ushna (Pungent) 5. Thiktha (Bitter) 6. Kashaya (Astringent)	3. Katu (Pungent/hot)

Table. 35 Vipaka

Earlier we discussed the role of six *rasa* in metabolism. The role of *vipaka* can make it clearer. Let us see how *Vipaka* determine the metabolic activity of a dravya.

Three Vipaka

1. Why six rasa are biotransformed to only **three** vipaka?
2. Why they are named same as *rasa?*
3. Why *Lavana* (Salty), *Thiktha* (Bitter) and *Kashaya* (Astringent) are out of the scene?

1. This is probably to tally with the magic numeric of *tridosha.* So **Vipaka triad.**
2. *Rasa* represent the perceivable property of food and medicine. Vipaka is therapeutically *active rasa.*
3. *Madhura* (Sweet), *Amala* (Sour Acidic) and *Katu* (Pungent) are more suitable to represent *Kapha, Pitha and Vata* respectively

Consider three stages in digestion.

(1) Early stage (in mouth) –where *Kapha dosha* is prominent

(2) Middle stage (in stomach) - where *Pitha dosha* is prominent

(3) Final stage (in intestine) – where *Vata dosha* is prominent

Rasa (Taste)	Biotransformation (vipaka) at	Vipaka	Affected dosha
Madhura (Sweet) Lavana(Salty)	Mouth	Madhura (Sweet)	Kapha
Amla (Sour)	Stomach	Amla (Sour)	Pitha
Katu (Pungent) Thikta (Bitter) Kashaya (Astringent)	Intestines (Small & Large)	Katu	Vata

Table. 36 Rasa, vipaka and affected dosha

Both *shad rasa* (six tastes) and *tridosha* have *Panchamahabhoota* constitution, so also *Vipaka*, the '*rasa transformed product'*. This explains the therapeutic influence of *vipaka* on tridosha.

Madhura Vipaka

In Madhura rasa (Sweet) *Prithwi* (earth element) and *Ap* (water element) are prominent. Biotransformed to *madhura vipaka* in digestion no change occurs in its *panchamahabhoota* combination.

But *Lavana rasa* (salty taste), with prominence in *Ap* and *Agni* (fire element) when changed to *madhura vipaka* its *Agni* element is compromised for *prithwi* . This is a condition of two *rasa* changing to one *vipaka*

The diagrams are for i llustration only. Consider the five coloured circles as *pachamahabhoota*. The biggest one represent the actively prominent element and smaller circles functionally obscure. According to Ayurveda every matter (*padhartha*) is a combination of all the five elements.

Madhura rasa & Lavana rasa ⟶ Madhura Vipaka ⟶ (influence) Kapha dosha

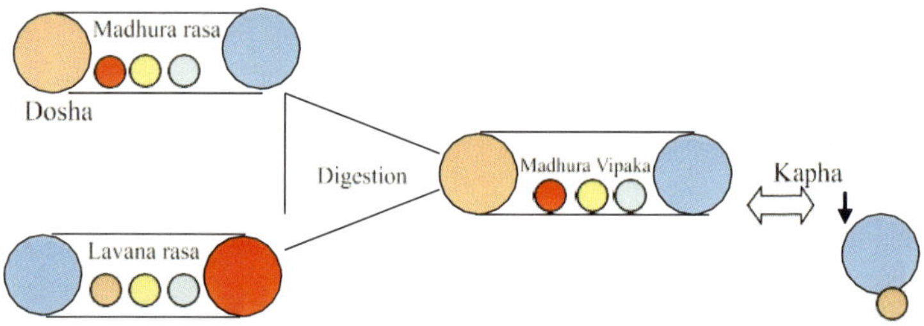

Amla Vipaka

In *Amla rasa* (sour taste), *Prithwi* (earth element) and *Agni* (fire element) are prominent. No changes occur in Panchamahabhoota combination when changed to *Amala Vipaka* after digestion. In this case one *rasa* change to one *vipaka.*

Amla rasa ⟶ Amla Vipaka ⟶ (influence) Pitha dosha

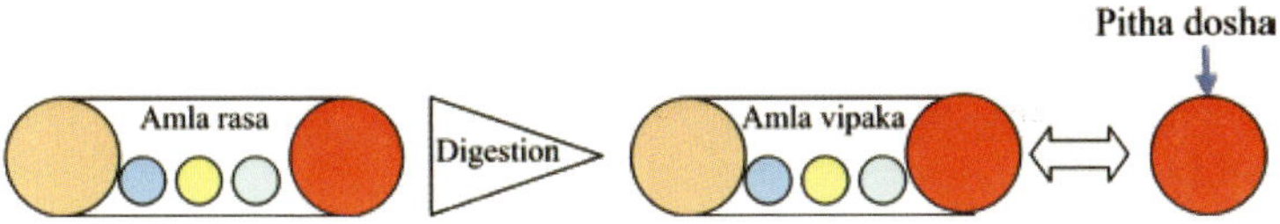

Katu Vipaka

Thikta rasa (bitter taste), *Katu rasa* (pungent taste) and *Kashaya rasa* (astringent taste) are transformed to *Katu vipaka*. During this process elemental combination of *Katu rasa* (pungent taste) is preserved.

In *Thiktha rasa* (bitter taste), *Vayu* (air element) and *Akash* (ether element) are prominent. During the change to *katu vipaka*, *Akas* (ether element) is compromised for Agnibhuta (fire element).

Kashaya rasa (astringent taste) is prominent in *Prithwi* (earth element) and *Vayu* (air element). During the change to *katu vipaka*, P*rithwi* (earth element) is compromised for *Agni* (fire element). Here three *rasa* transform to one Vipaka

Tiktha, Katu & Kashaya rasa ⟶ Katu vipaka ⟶ Vata dosha

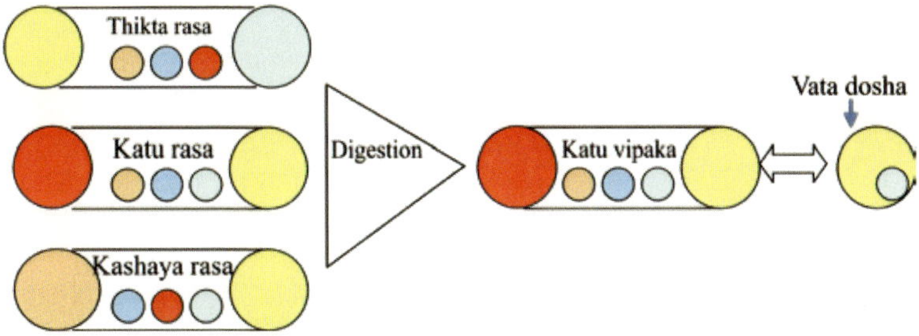

Digestion

Most of the organic molecules that are ingested are similar to the molecules that form human tissues. These are usually large molecules (polymers), which are composed of subunits (monomers). Digestion is the process by which these large molecules are converted to monomers by means of hydrolysis reaction and are transported across the wall of the small intestine in to the blood and lymph in the process of absorption. Centuries old Ayurveda is ignorant of the biomolecules .

According to Ayurveda there are three types of digestive energies

(1)Jadaragni (2) Bhutagni and (3) Dhaatwagni

1. Jadaragni: Let us compare Jadaragni with the digestive enzymes in the Gastro intestinal tract (*Koshta*). In gastrointestinal tract different areas have different digestive phases. Ayurveda mentioned the stages of digestion as *'Avastha Paka'* (Paka = digestion, Avasta = Stage). The different stages of digestion occur in mouth, stomach, duodenum and intestine.

Mechanical digestion begin in the mouth as food is chewed. Food in the mouth is in 'Amavastha' (*Ama* means incompletely digested and *avastha*, the stage) with 'Madhura Vipaka' (Sweet). In the stomach and duodenum (grahani), combined with digestive enzymes it is in 'Pachyamanavastha' (digesting stage) and in 'Amla Vipaka' (Acidic). The final fate in the intestine is 'Pakwastha' (completely digested) and it will be in 'Katu Vipaka' (pungent).

<u>The modern aspect of digestion</u>

The masticated food is mixed with saliva that contains salivary amylase or ptylin, the enzyme that catalyze the partial digestion of starch. When reached in stomach it is churned and mixed with hydrochloric acid and protein digesting enzyme pepsin to form the chyme.

Proteins are only partly digested in the stomach by the action of the pepsin, while carbohydrates and fats are not digested at all by the pepsin. Amylase that initiated the digestion of starch in the mouth becomes inactivated in the stomach by the strong acidity of the gastric juice. The complete molecule of the food digestion occurs later, when the chyme enters the small intestine.

The digestion of starch mainly occurs in the duodenum (grahani) as a result of action of the pancreatic amylase. Straight chains of starch are cleaved to form disaccharide *maltose* and the trisaccharide *maltriose.* Pancreatic amylase, however cannot hydrolyze the bond between the glucose molecules at the branch point in the starch. As a result, short, branched chains of glucose molecules called *oligosaccharides* are formed.

Most of the protein digestion occurs in the duodenum and jejunum. That initiated in the stomach with the action of pepsin liberates some amino acids in the stomach. Here it helps to produce a more homogenous chyme. The complete digestion of protein occurs in the small intestine. The pancreatic enzymes *trypsin, chymotripsin and elastase* cleaves the peptide bonds in the interior of the polypeptide chains. These enzymes are called *endopeptidases.* Enzymes that remove amino acids from the ends of polypeptide chains, by contrast, are called as *exopeptidases.* Eg. *Carboxypeptidase* and the brush border enzyme *aminopeptidase.* The former removes amino acids from the carboxyl-terminal end of polypeptide chains and the later cleaves amino acids from the amino-terminal end of the polypeptide chains.

The arrival of the lipids (triglyceride or fat) in the duodenum stimulates the secretion of bile. Bile salt micelles are secreted in to the duodenum and act to break up the fat droplets into tiny *emulsification droplets* of triglyecides. Fat digestion occurs at the surface of droplets through the enzymatic action of *pancreatic lipase.*

Thus food in the duodenum (grahani) is in Pachyamanavastha, the digesting stage. When food is in the intestine, it is in Pakwavastha- the digested stage. Carbohydrates, lipids, amino acids, calcium and iron are absorbed in the duodenum and jejunum. Bile salts, Vitamin B12 water and electrolytes are absorbed primarily in the ileum.

Food/drug in	Stages of digestion	Vipaka
Mouth	Amavastha (Incompletely digested)	Madhura (Sweet phase)
Stomach	Pachyamanavastha (Digesting)	Amla (Acidic phase)
Intestine	Pakwavastha (Digested)	Katu (Pungent)

Table. 37 Stages of digestion (Avastha paka)

Nishta Paka (the destined digestion)

The final biotransformation of the ingested substance (food or drug) attained through the effects of *rasa, guna, veerya, vipaka and prabhava* is called as *Nishta paka.* (Nishta = destined). It is the conclusive metabolic or therapeutic effect.

Diagrammatic representation of Nishta paka

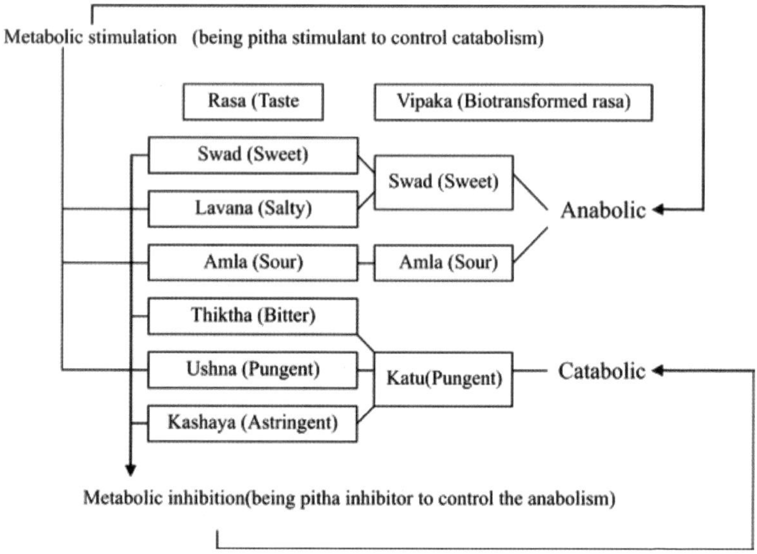

2. Panchamahabhootagni

Let us consider Panchamahabhoota in two categories.

a. The non- corporeal elements - those elements prior to the formation of the body tissues (*Ashareer Mahabhoot*)

b. The corporeal elements -those which constitute the body tissues (*Shareer Mahabhoot*)

The energy needed to change the noncorporeal elements to the corporeal elements is *Panchamahabhootagni*. According to this concept each Panchamahabhoota has specific energy (*Agni*). For example, when we drink water (Ap/ Jala), Jalamahabhoot-agni transforms the water to Shareera jala (the body fluids).

3. Dhaatwagni

There are seven *Dhaatu (*Tissue) as explained earlier. Each one is the precursor of the next and has specific *Agni* (energy) for transforming to the next. This represents successive formation of tissues.

PRABHAVA

Definition of *Prabhava*: It is the therapeutic quality of a drug which is not expected from it or not destined on it. The Sanskrit word can have any one the following meanings:

1. Influence
2. Effect
3. Impact
4. Unprecedented effect.

Pharmacodynamics of Ayurveda was explained above with the concepts of *Rasa* (Taste), *Guna* (Quality), *Veerya* (Potency) and *Vipaka* (bio-transformation). At times a drug may act by a different way, not explained by any one of the above category. This specific effect of a drug might be due to an innate power of that drug. That is *Prabhava*. Therapeutic actions of few medicinal plants are compared to explain this phenomenon.

Example 1

As per *rasa, guna, veerya*, and *vipaka* therapeutic qualities of *Plumbago rosea* (Chithraka) and *Operculina turpethum* (Nagadanti) are same. Pulmbago is carminative, but Operculina Turpethum is purgative. According to Ayurveda this is due to *Prabhava.*

Medicinal plant	Ayurveda Pharmacodynamic concepts				Action
	Rasa	Guna	Veerya	Vipaka	
Plumbago Rosea (Chitraka)	Katu (Pungent)	Laghu (light) Rooksha (dry) Theek-shna (Potent)	Ushna (hot)	Katu (pungent)	Digestive-Carminative
Operculina Turpethum (Nagadanti)	Same	Same	Same	Same	Purgative

Table. 38 Example of Prabhava (i)

Example 2: *Vitis Vinifera* (grapes) and *Glycyrrhiza glabra* (Licorice)

Vitis Vinifera is laxative due to Prabhava even though both have same Ayurvedic pharmacological qualities.

Medicinal plant	Ayurveda Pharmacodynamic concepts				Action
	Rasa	Guna	Veerya	Vipaka	
Vitis Vinifera (grapes)	Madhura (Sweet)	Snigdha(Oily) Guru Heavy) Mridu (Soft)	Sheetha (Cool)	Madhura (Sweet)	Laxative
Glycyrrhiza glabra (Yashti madhu)	Same	Same	Same	Same	Expectorant Demulcent Antiulcerant

Table. 39 Example of Prabhava (ii)

Ayurveda pharmaceutics is known as *Bhaishajya kalpana*. '*Oushadha yoga*'- the drug combinations and therapeutic applications are in Sanskrit poems (*sloga*) with meter and melody! Poetry was known to serve as a memory aid. Each poetic *yoga* (the combinations) mentions names of the medicinal plants, minerals, additives, mode of preparation and diseases (sometimes many) for which it can be prescribed. Physicians recollect the Sanskrit *sloga* (poems) explaining the therapeutic action before prescribing!

Herbal drugs are commonly prescribed and consumed as the extract of the whole fresh herb(s), decoctions of single or combination herbs, herbal tea, tablets, powders and topical applications. Metallic and non metallic substances are subjected to a ritualistic purification by calcination with herbal extracts or cattle urine with cow pats as the fuel. This purification process is supposed to make the heavy metals non toxic.

Internationally accepted monitoring authorities and guidelines have to be developed to monitor worldwide research and development of herbal medicine.

Many plants contain active compounds that are as strong as those found in any modern drug, but they also contain other chemicals that modify the dominant compound's effect, thus making some herbal remedies gentle and less toxic than prescription drugs when used as directed. Ayurveda pharmacological terminologies noted above are not sufficient to explain and explore the medically active content of the medicinal plants.

Therapeutic effect of medicinal plants is due to its phytochemical contents. There are thousands of different phytochemicals and many studies about the health benefits of phytochemicals are being carried out to explore the invaluable reservoir of new bioactive molecules. For example, a study on Chithraka (Plumbago rosea) referred from the published papers is cited below.

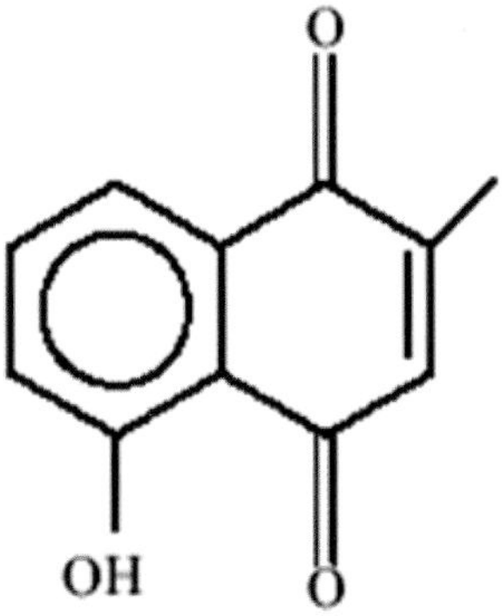

In animal studies, plumbagin, napthoquinone from *Plumbago rosea* (Chitraka) has shown anti tumour activity. The anti tumour and radiomodifying properties of plumbagin were tested on mouse Ehrlich ascites carcinoma in animal model. Plumbagin produced inhibition of exponentially growing tumours. When radiation was combined with plumbagin, mouse survival was increased by 120 days. Result indicate that ethanolic extract of PZ Linn. possess significant anticancer activity and also reduce elevated level of lipid peroxidation due to higher content of terpinoiods and flavonoids. (Int.J Bioed Res 1 (2), 1-9, 2010.)

The efficacy of a drug can be significantly affected by the method of drug delivery. The slowness in the efficiency of a treatment suggest a growing need for a specialty approach to the delivery of drugs to specific targets in the body. Hence an efficient delivery system that can deliver optimum amount of drug to the site of action has to be developed for herbal medicine to make a successful bid in the treatment of various human ailments.

Ayurveda students must learn phytochemistry and pharmacology for a better service with Ayurveda.

Science is never old always!

CHAPTER 6

The Mind - in health and disease

Ayurveda and Modern perspective

Ayurveda is strongly rooted in a 'mind-body' concept.

According to Maharshi Charaka, mind (*manas*) is known as *Satwa* or *Chetah* (bearer of capability of thinking).

Mind cannot be perceived by sense organs, *it is Atindriya* or super sense. It connects sense organs with the intellect. It is known as *Satwa* (the essence) or *Chetah* (the consciousness). Its functions depend up on i ts objects and consciousness in the same axis and it is the cause of activity of all other sense organs (Ch. Su. 8.4).

According to Charaka, the presence of cognition as well as the absence of cognition constitutes an indication of m ind. The functions of the mind are directions of s enses (*Indriyabhigrah*), control of itself (*Manonigraha*), reasoning (*Ooham*) and deliberation (*Vichara*) – (Ch. Sh. 1.21).

The object interaction is possible through the bio-energy which Charaka termed as 'Vayu' (Ch. Su. 12-18). Sense organs are capable of perceiving their respective objects at the instance of m ind (Ch. Su. 8.7). According to him, *self* is active and that by *its* activity the mind moves; and it is by the operation of m ind that the senses move. The self is *conscious*, but this consciousness does not belong to the self in itself, it is attained only by its connection with the senses through the *manas* (Ch. Su. 1.47).

Charaka recognized the interdependence and inseparable relationship of mind and body. Pleasure, pain and the movements involved in thought process are attributed to *manas* which drives its activity from the self. The harmonious or concordant inter-action between the mind and body is the cause of wellbeing (Ch. Su. 1.55). The erroneous, inadequate or e xcessive interaction between body and mind due to many factors including periodic climate change (*Kala*); psychic repercussion (*Budhi*) and transgression of the bounds of moderation and agreeability relatively to one's nature and capacity (*Indriyartha*) are bound to lead to psychosomatic strain and discordance resulting in disease (Ch. Su 1.54).

Ayurveda consider three philosophical attributes as *guna* (qualities) of mind - Satwa, Raja and Tama (Table 4). The action of mind is determined by the quality of soul (Atma), like happiness, misery etc. Mind acts as the driving force for all the sense faculties. Though mind does so many actions swiftly, there is no multiplicity of mind, it is one and only one. In an individual, the mind appears to have multiple characters due to its various actions, perception of the objects of sense faculties (*Swa Artha*); its dispositions, determination, swift association with sense organs to receive knowledge, and association with its qualities (*Sankalpa Vyabhicharana*).

Rigveda is the first available document of Indian literature in which mythological and religious meaning is attached to mental health and illness. This treaty is followed by the Adharvaveda wherein one finds the concept of mental health in terms of blessing from the Gods and that of the mental illness as the curse of Gods.

In another study Adharvavedic concept on the mental illness was viewed as an act of post session by a demon or divine agent, sorcery and witches, an effect of an evil eye cast on individual and a curse of defied souls of departed ancestors (Balodhi and Chowdhuri 1986). These concepts must have been flourished for several centuries and a mass of such thoughts would have accumulated.

It was the inherent heterogeneity of this material that led to its systematization. It is, now, difficult to ascertain the chronology, names and detail of persons who might have contributed to medicine and its systematization. The oldest available books now are 'Charaka Samhita (400 BC), 'Susruta Samhita' ((500 BC) and 'Kashyapa Samhita' 200 BC)

We have much to learn how psychological factors affect physical disorders and disease. The same kind of causal factors active in psychological disorders – social, psychological and biological – play a role in some physical disorders.

According to Ayurveda a destabilized mind also subvert Tridosha. But the challenge is to explain how a supposedly non-material mind influence a material body and vice-versa. Here the factor attracting the most attention is stress. You can have a certain type of personality or psychological make up that predisposes you to develop a specific kind of disorder.

Long unabated stress precipitates the original condition in to a real illness. If you have a family history of hypertension, for example, and you are under a constant level of stress at your job your blood pressure is slightly elevated. Suddenly, if one or more stressful life events take place your blood pressure might zoom up to an alarmingly high point.

Following are two clinically relevant references.

i. In 1936 Hans Selye, a young scientist noticed that one group of rats he injected with certain chemical extracts developed ulcers and other physiological problems, including atrophy of immune system issues. But a control group of rats who received a daily saline injection that should not have had any effect developed the *same* physical problems. Selye pursued this unexpected finding and discovered that the daily injections themselves seemed to be the culprit rather than the injected substance. (Abnormal Psychology/9/Physical disorders and health psychology-Barlow/Durand)

ii. (1) *Doshairvyasthaisamasthaischa* ***Bhayachoka****acha shadvidha:*

Athisara...... (A.H. S.8/1)

(2) Mithyaharaviharena visheshena virodhina

Sadhunindavadhaanyaswaharana*daischa seveithai.....* (A.H S 14/1)

The first Sanskrit verse above, is about the etiology *(nidana)* of di arrhea. There, apart from the causes vitiating Tridosha, **fear (*bhaya*)** and **distress (*shoka*)** are also mentioned as etiology of diarrhea.

The second verse is about the etiology of skin diseases. There also, apart from the vitiated Tridosha ***Contempt of poor people (Sadhu ninda)***, **murder (vadha)** and ***theft of other's properties (anyaswaharana)*** are the psychological factors in the etiology of skin diseases.

Relevant to the above Ayurveda examples of 'emotional factors triggering the physical illnesses' I might add a scientific study below.

'When you are nervous, you sweat. It is a common reaction and few would stop to contemplate the mechanism involved. But sweating in response to a stress is clear example of mind affecting body and, more specifically, of emotions manifesting through the skin. Psychologists and psychologically minded dermatologists have known for some time that emotional problems can trigger skin problems. Dr. Robert Griesemer, M.D., a Boston based dermatologist, finally confirmed it. Dr. Griesemer interviewed 4576 pa tients to determine whether they had experienced a particularly stressful event – a serious argument with someone they cared about, job, or school pressure, etc. – within the usual incubation period for their particular skin disorder.

His results were remarkable. He found that 94 percent of the people with acne -like symptoms and 95 pe rcent of the wart cases were set off by emotional factors. Some of the other ailments that ranked high on his "emotionally triggered" list include:

Psoriasis, 62 percent;

Hives. 68 percent,

Various types of eczema, 56 to 70 percent;

Pruritus or itching, 86 percent; and

Severe itching, 98 percent.

Mind/body techniques including biofeedback, hypnosis, and progressive relaxation techniques have been used to treat many of these problems with varying degrees of success. The use of hypnosis in the treatment of warts is perhaps the most documented' *(Ref: The complete guide to your emotions and health- a new dimensions in mind/body healing by Emrika Pandus/prevention magazine)*

Unmada (Psychosis)

Charaka define insanity as:

"Mano budhi satwa samnja smrithi

Bhakthi sheela cheshta vibhramasth 'unmadaha'

An abnormal state of mind, intelligence, quality, cognition, memory, devotion, habit, and activities is *Unmada* (Psychosis).

Fifteen types Unmanda are mentioned in the following table.

No	Ayurvedic name	Ayurvedic clinical symptoms translated to English
1	Vatonmada	Paradoxical laughter, inappropriate smile, abnormal involuntary movements, singing, zygomatic activity, involuntary movements with the limbs, crying, dry skin. Symptoms aggravate after the digestion of food.
2	Pithonmada	Impatience, abnormal involuntary movements, stripping*, threatening others, running, hot body*, anger or paranoia, affinity towards shadows*, cold food* and cold water* (*In a psychotic break the sudden onset of changes to neurotransmitters, hormones and blood pressure can make a person extremely hot. Alternatively when someone is in that state anything and everything in their immediate surroundings is irritating, right down to the clothes touching their skin. Given that they aren't properly " in their right mind" they lose contact with reality; (i.e., the part of their brain that would typically understand and observe social norms), and stripping of their clothes is an easy fix.)

No	Ayurvedic name	Ayurvedic clinical symptoms translated to English
3	Kaphonmada	Quiet, loss of taste, affinity towards women (? Satyriasis) **, liking loneliness, excess sleep, vomiting, Salivation, symptoms aggravate after food, pallor, white urine and stool.
4	Sannipadonmada	Symptoms of most severe condition of psychosis.
5	Shokonmada	Depression, Uttering secrets, contradictory senses, idiotic expressions in singing, laughing and lamenting.
6	Vishonmada	Reddish eyes, loss of strength, senses, and luster; livid face and inconsistent consciousness.
7	Bhootonmada	Clinical symptoms of the categories from 7 to 15 are not included. They include in the category of concept of mental health in terms of the blessings and curse of the Gods and by an act of the post session by a demon or divine agent, sorcery and witches, an effect of an evil eye cast on individual and a curse of defied souls of departed ancestors (as explained above).
8	Devagraha peedithonmada	
9	Asuragraha peedithonmada	
10	Gandharvagraha peedithonmada	
11	Yakshagraha peedithoada	
12	Pithrugraha peedithonmada	
13	Bhujangagraha peedithonmada	
14	Rakshasagraha peedithonmada	
15	Pishachagraha peedithonmada	

Table. 40 Types of Unmada (** I doubt the Kaphonmada in females may shows/o nymphomaniac)

The modern structure of Mind

Mind is 'the Psyche; the organ or seat of consciousness, remembering, reasoning and willing' (Stedman's Medical dictionary).

According to Freud, the mind has three major parts or functions:

1. The ***id***
2. The ***ego*** and
3. The ***superego***.

Id is the source of our strong sexual and aggressive feelings or energies. It is basically, the animal within us; if totally unchecked, it would be make us all rapist and killers. The energy or drive within *id* is the libido. The *id* operates according to the *pleasure principle* with an overriding goal of maximizing pleasure and eliminating any associated tension or c onflicts. The *id* has its own characteristic way of pro cessing information; referred to as *primary process*, this type of thinking is very emotional, irrational, illogical, filed with fantasies, and preoccupied with sex, aggression, selfishness and envy. Fortunately or all of us, according to Freud's view, the *id* is selfish and sometimes dangerous drive do not go unchecked.

The part of our mind that ensures that we act realistically is called, ***ego*** and it operates according the *reality principle* instead of the *pleasure principle*. The cognitive operations or t hinking style of e go re-characterized by logic and reason are referred to as the *secondary process*, opposite to that of *id*

The ***super ego***, what we might call *conscience* represents the *moral principles* instilled in us by our parents and our culture.

Psychopathology

Psychopathology is the study of psychological disorders. Etiology of psychic disorders includes, biological, psychological and social dimensions.

Emotion is a strong feeling, aroused mental state, or intense state of drive or unrest directed toward a definite object and evidenced in both behavior and psychologic changes (Stedman's Medical dictionary) Emotional influences contribute in a variety of ways to psychopathology, as do 'social and interpersonal' influences.

Modern treatment of psychological conditions

Knowing how the nervous system and, especially, the brain work is central to any understanding of our behavior, emotions, and cognitive processes. This is the focus of neuroscience. The biochemical neurotransmitters in the brain and nervous system that carry messages from one neuron to another are the area of intense attention by the psychopathologists.

Research on neurotransmitter functions focuses primarily on what happens when activity levels change. We can manipulate these activity levels with certain *substances* when it turns to psychopathological.

Substances that affectively *increase* the activity of a neurotransmitter by mimicking its effects are called **agonists**.

Substances that decrease or block, a neurotransmitter are called **antagonists** .

Substances that produce effects *opposite* to those produced by the neurotransmitter are called **inverse agonists.**

Serotonin, Gamma Aminobutyric Acid (GABA), Norepinephrine and Dopamine are few neurotransmitters that are important in psychopathology .

Relaxation and Meditation

Meditation and relaxation techniques decreases the effects of stress on our mind and body. In *progressive muscle relaxation*, devised by Edwin Jacobson in 1938, people become acutely aware of any tension in their bodies and counteract it by relaxing specific muscle groups. In *transcendental meditation,* attention is focused solely on a repeated syllable or the *mantra*

When in pain patients can either turn to prescription or turn on their music player to few minutes of soothing harp music and guided relaxations. There are incidents, some of the doctor's prescribing 'music tape' instead of pain killers and tranquilizers! It is being used before cardiac surgery, during chemotherapy and with patients with chronic back pain and crippling spinal injuries. In hospital's stress management center, the same music and relaxation training is used to treat many stress -related illness, including high blood pressure, migraine headaches, and ulcers.

Relaxation response is our protective mechanism against overreaction to stress. In stress response you escalate the sympathetic nervous system. In the relaxation response, you de-escalate the sympathetic nervous system. In stress response your pupils dilate, your hearing becomes more acute, your blood pressure increases, your heart rate increase, respiration rate increases, circulation changes and moves away from the periphery in to the muscles of vital organs and you become pale. These are just some of the physiological responses that may occur. The relaxation response is the opposite. People who regularly practice relaxation technique, like meditation are less anxious and tense and better able to resist stress. They are more optimistic, self-confident, energetic, and productive. Numerous studies confirm the profound effect of meditation has on lowering blood pressure and even cholesterol.

There are different techniques of relaxation like Transcendental Meditation (TM), Zen and Yoga, Autogenic training, Progressive relaxation and Hypnosis with Suggested sleep Relaxation.

CHAPTER 7

The importance of phytochemistry in Ayurveda

Interestingly, Ayurvedic medicine is practiced in a way similar to the biomedicine but using different forms of intervention and treatment – for instance, using herbs and herbo-minerals instead of prescription drugs.

Many people regard herbal medications as 'safe' because they are natural. This is neither rational nor true. Western trained doctors generally express significant anxiety over the potential for herbal medications to cause toxic injury although the pharmaceuticals they prescribe also have potentially lethal side effects. Correctly used, however, Ayurvedic therapies may be less toxic than prescription drugs.

The knowledge of chemistry of medicinal plants gives insight to the therapeutic and toxic properties of the component of the prescription. The claims on cure of medicines listed in historical texts is not genuinely sufficient to cure patients. We cannot trust the safety of the drugs simply because they are quotes from the old texts.

I strongly recommend inclusion of phytochemistry in the curriculum of Ayurveda course. Plants are complex mixtures of various compounds. One ingredient may be principally responsible for an action; where as other components may be important activators or modifiers of this action. We should know whether the interaction of a variety of compounds makes remedies safer and more effective. The continuing avalanche of information, made possible by technological innovations in biochemistry and molecular biology, now allows previously unimaginable insights into the inner working of living organisms and the cause of disease.

Chemistry of a plant is responsible for the Ayurvedic properties like *Rasa, Guna, Veerya, Vipaka and Prabhava.* Many of the powerful drugs used in modern medicines originated in plants. Following are few basic phytochemical contents of the plants that work as medicines in Ayurvedic medicine or modern medicine.

- Shikimic Acid
- Alkaloids
- Isoprenoids
- Polyketides
- Flavanoids
- Lignans
- Coumarins

- Glycosides
- Tannis
- Proteins
- Polysaccharides
- Fatty Acids
- Volatile oils and
- Vitamins.

SHIKIMIC ACID

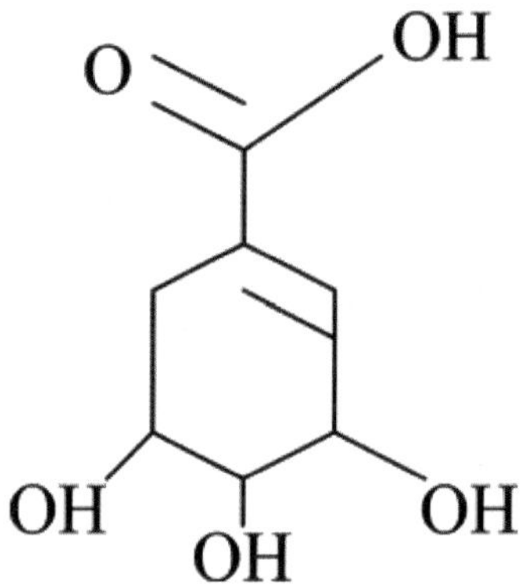

Shikimic acid is 3,4,5-trihydroxy-1-cyclohexene-1-carboxylic acid, an intermediate in the bacterial synthesis of phe nylalanine and tyrosine. It was first isolated from the Japanese flower *shikimi*, hence its name.

Shikimic Acid serves as the starting material for Oseltamivir (the active principle of Tamiflu) which is a neuraminidase inhibitor used in the treatment and prophylaxis of both influenza A and B

The active ingredient of the Chinese herb Illicium Verum Hook.f. (Star Anise) is Shikimic acid.

Shikimic Acid

Phosphoenol pyruvate (PEP) + Erythrose – 4 –Phosphate = **SHIKIMIC ACID**

Derivatives of Shikimic acid

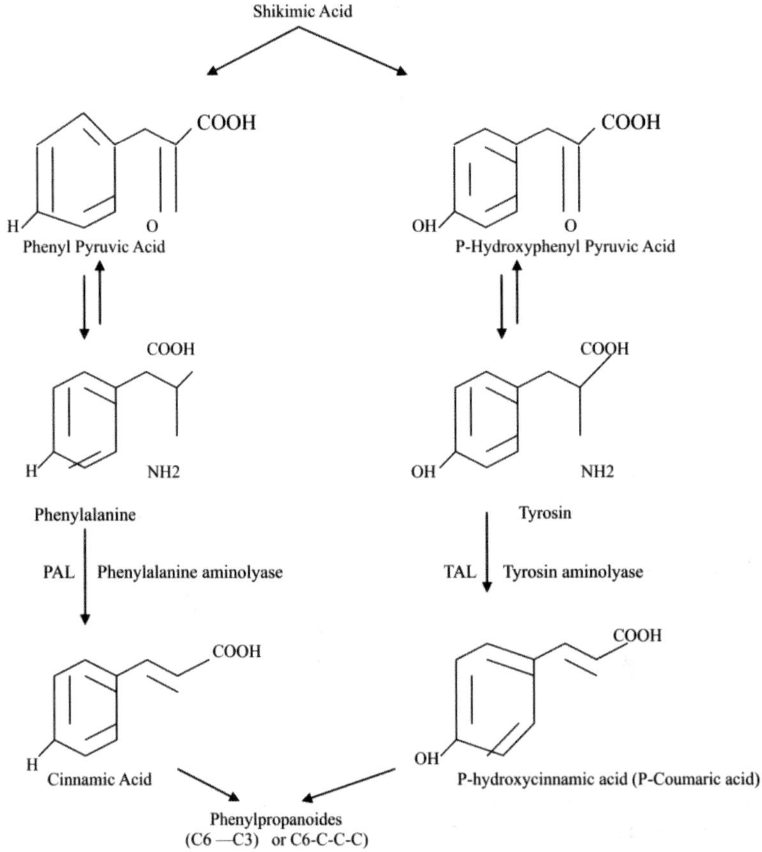

ALKALOID
S

Alkaloids are synthesized by the plant and are found in the leaf, bark, seed or other parts usually constituting the active principle of the crude drug. They are distinguished by basic reactions (hence the name) arising from heterocyclic nitrogen-containing complex structures. Although many alkaloids have profound physiological properties when consumed by animals, their roles in the plants are relatively obscure. Because they often have bitter tastes or are poisonous, alkaloids may protect plants against herbivores, insects and microbes. Over 5000 alkaloids have been isolated from plants. The term alkaloid was first coined by the German chemist Carl F. W. Meissner in1819 and the word is derived from the Arabic *al-qali*, a plant from which soda was first isolated.

Alkaloids are highly reactive substances with biological activity in low doses.

In the plants they may exist:

- in the free state
- as salts
- as N – Oxides

Properties of Alkaloids

1. Contain –nitrogen- usually derived from an aminoacid.
2. Bitter tasting, generally white solids (exception - nicotine is a brown liquid)
3. They give precipitate with heavy metal iodides.

- Most alkaloids are precipitated from neutral or slightly acidic solution by Mayer's reagent (Potassium Mercuric Iodide Solution). Cream coloured precipitate.
- Dragendoff's reagent (Solution of Potassium Bismuth Iodide) gives orange coloured precipitate with alkaloids.
- Caffein, a purine derivative, does not precipitate like most alkaloids.

4. Alkaloids are basic—they form water- soluble salts. Most alkaloids are well defined crystalline substances which unite with acids to form salts.
5. Occur in limited number of plants. Neuclic acid exists in all plants, where as, Morphine exists in only one plant species.

There are three main types of Alkaloids

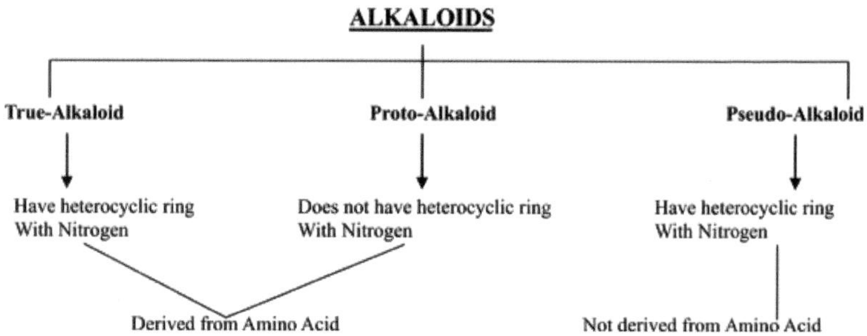

True Alkaloid: The basic units in the biogenesis of t he true alkaloids are Amino acids. The non-nitrogen containing rings or s ide chains are derived from Terpene units and/or Acetate, while Methionine is responsible for t he addition of methyle group to nitrogen atom.

Proto-Alkaloid: Colchicin is an example of a Proto-Alkaloid. It is obtained from colchicum and is used for gout.

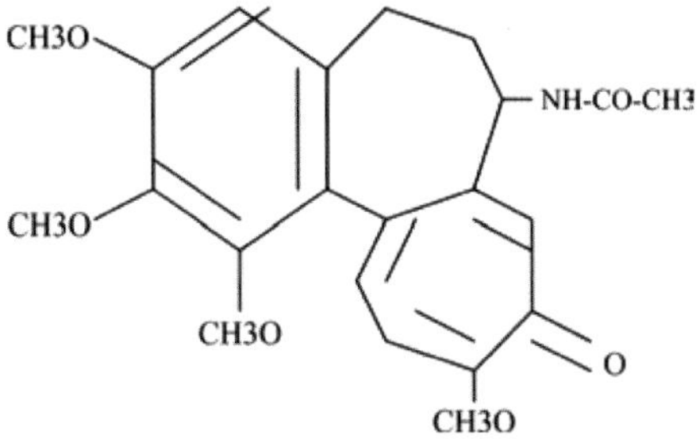

Colchecin from Tyrosin

Colchicine is a very old drug, which has been used to treat joint pain since the 6th century A.D. It has been used for centuries (approximately 2000 years) as an anti-inflammatory agent in the treatment of gouty arthritis.

Pseudo- Alkaloid: derived from

- Terpenoids or
- Purines

Egs: Caffeine (from Coffea arabica), Theobromine (from Theobroma cacao), Thephylline (from tea- Thea senensis)

Alkaloids can be classified:

- ☐ In terms of biological activity
- ☐ Chemical structure (Nucleus containing nitrogen) and
- ☐ Biosynthetic pathway (the way they are produced in the plants)

ALKALOIDS

ORNITHINE	TYROSIN	TRYPTOPHANE	PYRIDINE	LYSINE
↓	↓	↓	↓	↓
Tropane Pyrrolidine Pyrrolizidine	Benzyl-isoquinoline	Indole Quinolin	Pyridine	Quinolizidine Piperidine

TROPANEALKALOIDS

There are two important types of **Tropane alkaloids**

Tropane alkaloids

SOLANACEOUS ALKALOID		COCA ALKALOID	
Atropine	Hyoscyamine	Hyoscine	Cocaine

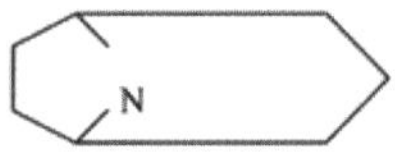

They have TROPANE NUCLEUS in common.

Bicyclic system made up of a 5-membered ring (1, N, 5, 6, and 7) and a 6-membered ring (1, 2, 3, 4, 5, N) N is common to both. The nucleus always carries oxygen in position 3.

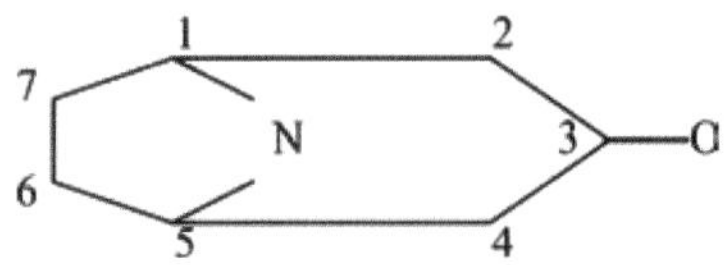

The Nitrogen is always methylated. The Oxygen is substituted with an aromatic acid, therefore, creating an ester

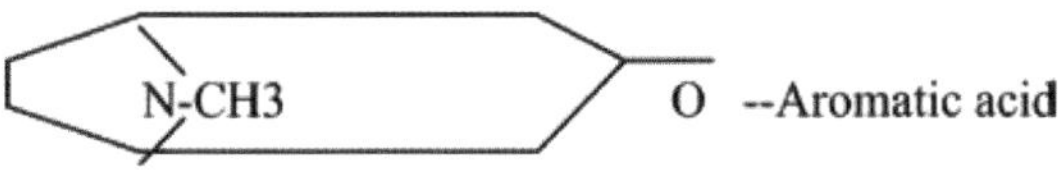

Solanaceous alkaloids come from the plants of Solanaceae, a family of plants that includes the genus Solanum. Eg. Lycopersicon Esculentum (Tomato), Solanum tuberosum (Potato).

Tomatin (LYCORSICIN) C50H83NO21 is a mixture of glycosides present in the leaves and stems of tomato plants; partial hydrolysis yields α -tomatine (the major constituent) β– tomatin, β 2- tomatin, γ- tomatin, and δ- tomatine. α – tomatine is made up of 1 mol of tomatidine linked to a tetrasaccharide (2 mols of D glucose, 1 mole of D-xylose, and 1 mol of D- galactose). It has antifungal and anti-inflammatory properties; is capable of antagonsing bradykinin and other substances believed to involve in the development of allergic reactions; and is used as a precipitating agent for steroids, as an alternative to digitonin. Digitonin is a steroid glycoside obtained from *Digitalis Purpurea.*

There are three sources of Solanaceous alkaloids.

1. BELLADONNA Eg. Plant: Atropa Belladonna (Deadly nightshade)
2. HYOSCIAMINES Eg. Plant: Hyoscyamus Niger (Henbane)
3. STRAMONIUM Eg. Plant: Datura stramonium (Jamestwon weed)

Hyoscine is the pure optical isomer, (+) Hyosciamine, (-) Hyosciamine. Atropine is the recemic of Hyosciamine.

Atropine = (+ -) Hyosciamine

The 3 – hydroxy derivative of Tropane is known as TROPINE.

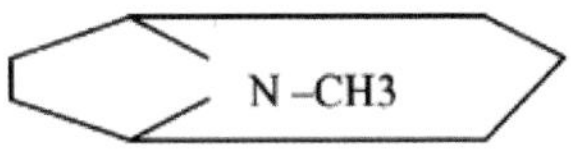

TROPANE

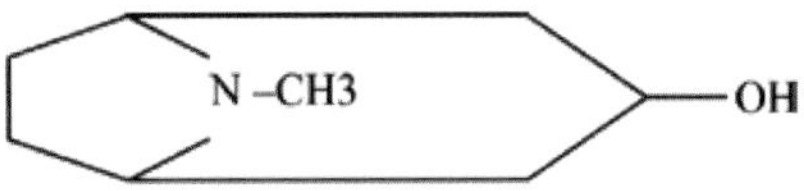

TROPINE

Esterification of Tropine with Tropic acid yields Hyoasciamine (Tropine tropate).

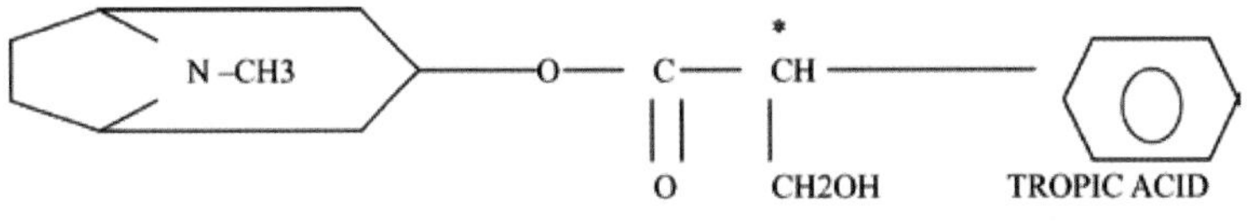

***Asymetric Center**

Ayurveda specifies the changes in the therapeutic values of plants collected during different seasons. The plants produce the pure optically active form (Hyosciamin) or t he mixture –recemic (Atropine) form depending on t he period of year (weather).

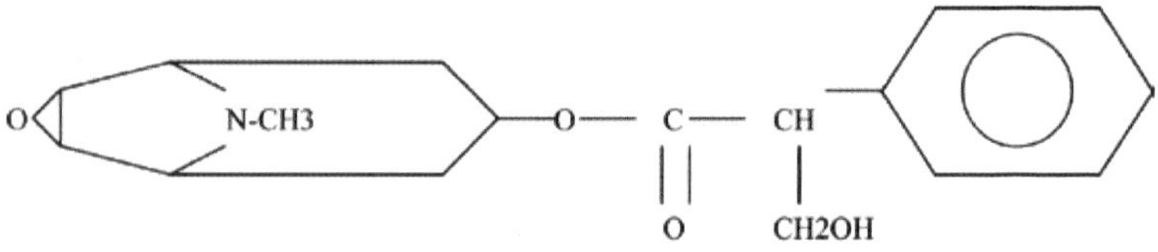

Hyosciamine.

Pharmacological importance of solaneous alkaloids :

Atropine: The alkaloid obtained from *Atropa belladonna*

- Antispasmodic
- Antisudorific
- Anticholinergic
- Mydriatic.

Hyosciamine: Daturine, duboisine, atropine tropate, alkaloid found in hyascyamus

- Antispasmodic
- Analgesic
- Sedative.

Hyoscine: Scopolamine, Atroscine, Scopine tropate; an alkaloid found in the leaves and seeds of Hyoscyamus niger, Duboisia myoproides, Scopolia japonica, Scopolia carniolica, Atropa belladonna and other solanaceous plants.

- Anticholinergic
- Mild analgesic
- Sedative, used in obstetrics to produce twilight sleep.

Stramonium: Jamestown or Jimson weed, Datura stramonium etc. contain an alkaloid, daturine, identical with hyoscyamine.

- Antispasmodic. Has been used in the treatment of asthama and parkinsonism
- When abused or taken inadvertently may cause an atropine -like toxic psychosis.

COCAINE

Coca or Coca leaves have been described as the dried leaves of Erythroxylum Coca. The plants are shrubs or small trees that attain a height of about 2 meters and are indigenous to certain areas of South America. The plant needs a very high altitude. Most of the present day supply of the drug is obtained from the activated plants grown at an altitude of 500 -2000 meters, in Peru and Bolivia.

The leaves are picked like tea and dried. The dried leaves contain about 1% total alkaloid. The alkaloids have the same tropane nucleus called ECGONINE.

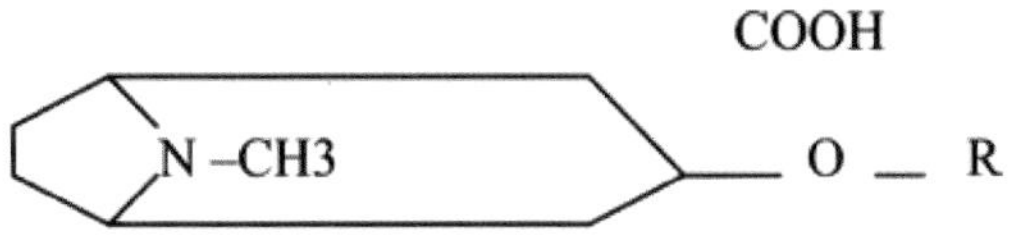

ECGONINE

R = Benzoid acid
= Cinnamic acid
= Cinnamic acid dimers.

PYRROLIDINE is Tetrahydropyrrole, pyrrole to which four H atoms have been added, basis of proline and Hydroxyproline.

PYRROLIZIDINE alkaloid is poisonous. The plants most frequently implicated in pyrrolizidine poisoning are members of Borginaceae, Compositae, and Leguminosae families. They contain over 100 hepatotoxic pyrrolizidine alkaloids. Pyrrolizidine alkaloid intoxication is caused by consumption of plant materials containing alkaloid. The plants may be consumed as food, for medicinal purposes, or as contaminants of agricultural crops. Cereal crops and forage crops are sometimes contaminated with pyrrolizzidine producing weeds, and the alkaloid find their way to flour and other foods, including milk from cows feeding on these plants.

All humans believed to be susceptible to the hepatotoxic pyrrolizidine alkaloid. Home remedies, and consumption of herbal tea in large quantities can be a risk factor. Most pyrrolizidine alkaloid toxicity results in moderate to severe liver damage. Gastro intestinal symptoms are usually the first sign of intoxication, then complaints of abdominal pain with vomiting and development of a scites. Evidence of the toxicity may not become apparent until sometimes after the alkaloid is ingested. Acute illness has been compared to the Budd-Chiari Syndrome (Thrombosis of he patic vein leading to hepatomegaly, portal hypertension and ascites.)

BENZYLEISOQUINOLIN (BIQ Alkaloids)

About 4000 BIQ alkaloids are known. There are many important structural types. Many BIQ alkaloids are important in medicine. Others are highly toxic. Some are used as arrow poisons. BIQ alkaloids are found in a number of related families and a few others. They are found in the Annonaceae, Aristolochiaceae, Berberidaceae, Eupomatiaceae, Hernandiaceae, Fabaceae, Fumariaceae, Lauraceae, Magnoliaceae, Menispermaceae, Monimiaceae, Nelumbonaceae, Papaveraceae, Ranunculaceae, Winteraceae, Euphorbiaceae (*Croton*), Rhamnaceae, Phellinaceae, Symplocaceae, Rutaceae, Combretaceae, Araliaceae, Apiaceae, Caprifoliaceae, Rubiaceae, and Araceae. Sanguinarine, the alkaloid from the plant Sanguinaria canadensis has been used a traditional drug, which has antimicrobial activity with broad range spectrum.

Few plants containing BIQ alkaloid

Papaver somniferum - opium poppy - Papaveraceae - flowers, fruit and sap.

Sanguinaria Canadensis - bloodroot - papaveraceae - root and plant with flower.

Ruta graveolens - Rutaceae - plant with flower and fruit.

Nelumbo lutea – yellow lotus - Nelumbonaceae - plant with flowers.

INDOLEALKALOIDS

The Indole system can be considered to consist of a Pyrole ring and Benzine ring fused together to form two isomeric Benzopyrrols, INDOLE AND ISO-INDOLE.

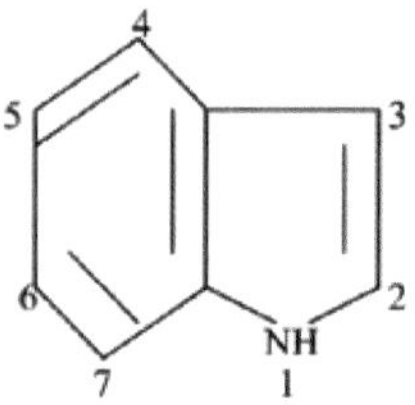

INDOLE

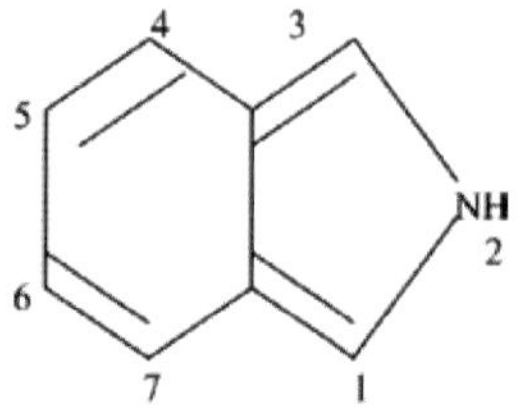

ISOINDOLE

The indole itself appears to be an essential constituent of the perfumes of flowers such as jasminium and of the citrus species. With respect to their structural features, the indole attached can be divided in to two main classes.

- The first class is that of the simple indole alkaloid.
- The indole alkaloid of the second class contains two structure- elements.

1. Tryptamine with the indole nucleus and
2. A C9 or C10 monoterpene moiety, derived from SECOLOGANIN.

INDOLE ALKALOID

Simple INDOLE NECLEUS

INDOLE NUCLEUS (from Tryptamine]
SECOLOGANIN (from Monoterpene)

The Indole alkaloid derived from tryptamine and secologanin can be classified to eight types, according to the structural characteristics of the skeleton

1. Corynanthean or C –type (Sarpaine, yohimbine, ajmalicine)
2. Vincosan or D type (vincoside)
3. Vallesiachotamon or V – type (vallesiachotamine)
4. Strychnan or S – type (vomicine)
5. Aspidospermatan or A – type (condylocarpine)
6. Eburnan or E – type (vincamine)
7. Plumeran or P – type (kopsine)
8. Ibogan or J – type (voaluteine)

More than a thousand alkaloids are derived by combining tryptane, tryptophan or dopamine moiety with amine or ten-carbon unit in various forms. The most common being the:

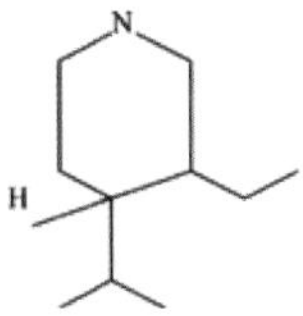

Corynanthean

As in the hetero –yohimbine ajmalicine

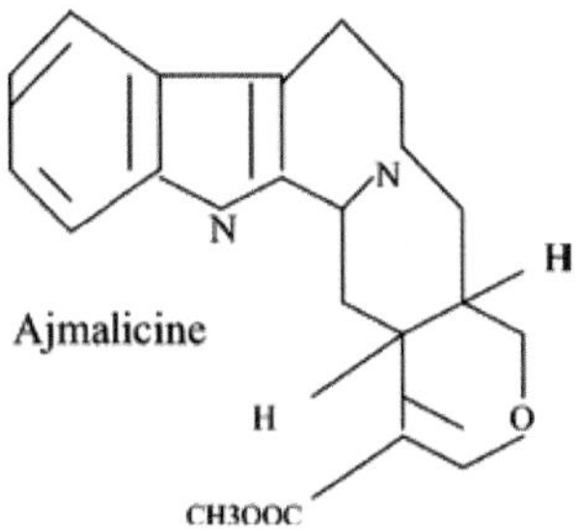

Ajmalicine

Or Emetine

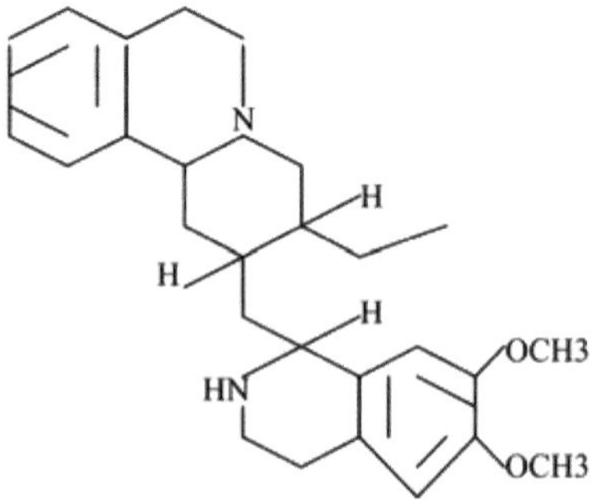

Emetine

The C9/C10 unit was found to be monoterpenoid in origin – the iridoid glucoside SECOLOGANIN

SECOLOGANIN

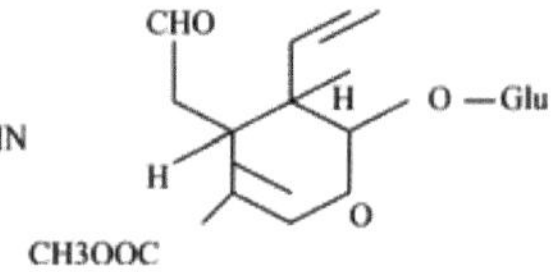

The main division of the Indole alkaloids can be found in:

RAUWOLFIA	**VINCA**	**ERGOT**		**PHYSOSTIGMA**
RESERPINE	VIMBLASTINE VINCRISTINE	ERGONOVINE	ERGOTOXINE ERGOTAMINE	PHYSOSTIGMINE ESERINE
		Water soluble	Water insoluble	

RAUWOLFIA ALKALOIDS

For centuries the natives of the Himalayan foothills have used the root of Rauwolfia for healing afflictions ranging from snakebite to insanity. Reserpine is the most important constituent.

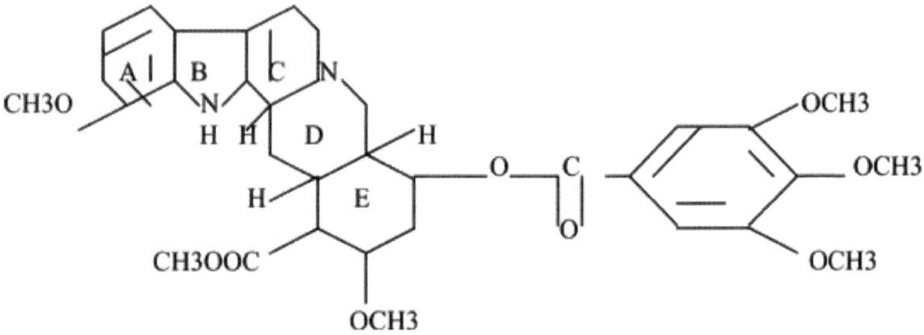

Reserpine depletes adrenergic vesicles of their transmitters, thereby, reducing amount of neurotransmitter released. This causes hypotension, bradycardia, increased gastrointestinal motility and increased rate of defecation. It also has a tranquillization effect but has been superseded by the Benzodiazapams.

The original source was from Rauwolfia serpentina from India. Major source at present is Rauwolfia Vomitoria from West Africa.

The basic ring system of nearly all Rauwolfia alkaloids are represented in the following four compounds.

7. Yohimbine, an alpha 2 adrenergic blocking agent and a serotinin antagonist
8. Ajimalicine
9. Ajimaline
10. Sarpagine

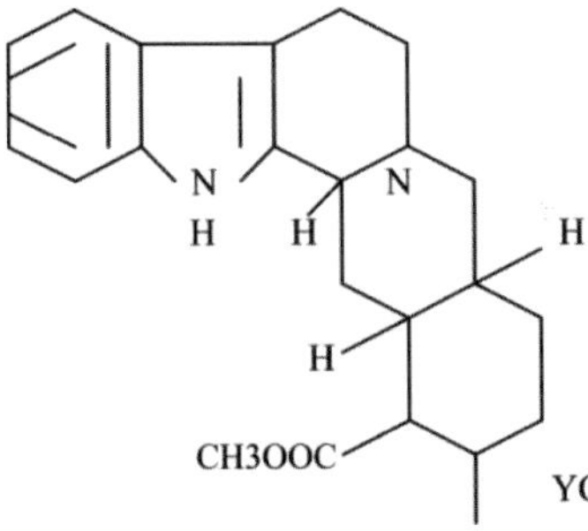

YOHIMBINE

VINCAROSEA (Catharanthus) (Medagascar Periwinkle)

The widespread reference in the folklore of the oral hypoglycaemic properties of leaf extracts from Catharanthus rosens prompted investigators which led to the discovery of D IMERIC INDOLE – dihyroindole alkaloid, VIMBLASTINE and VINCRISTINE. These alkaloid produced severe leukopenia in rats suggesting an anti-cancer potential especially for the treatment of leukemia.

These alkaloids are a dimer of CATHARANTHINE and VINDOLINE.

Catharanthine

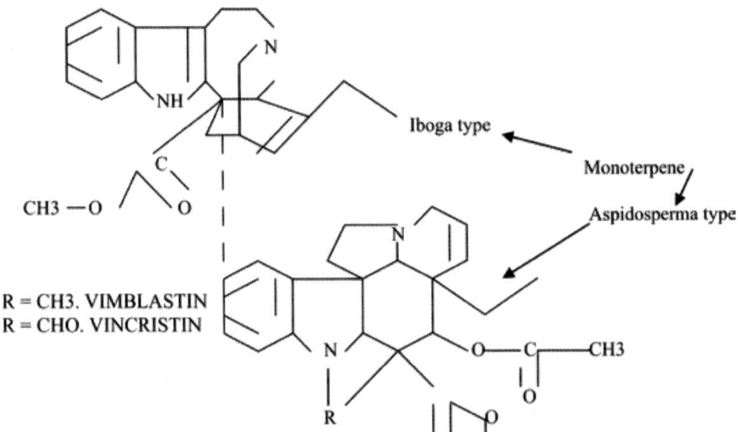

Vindolin

ERGOT

The sclerotium of the fungus *Claviceps purpurea,* a horny, elongated, blackish purple mass of peculiar disagreeable odor which replaces the grain of rye (*Secale cereale)* attacked by this fungus. It causes contraction of the muscular coat of the arteries, raising blood pressure, and contraction of the uterine muscles.

Ergonovine is an alkaloid from the ergot; on hydrolysis it yields D-lysergic acid and L-2-aminopropanol.

Ergotoxine is a mixture of alkaloids obtained from ergot, consisting of 1:1:1 mixture of ergocristine, ergocrinine and ergokryptine. It is a potent stimulant of the smooth muscle, particularly of the blood vessels and the uterus, and produce adrenergic blockade (chiefly of the alpha receptors). It is more toxic than the other natural and semisynthetic ergot alkaloids.

Ergotamine $C_{33}H_{35}N_5O_5$ is also an alkaloid from the ergot. It is also a potent stimulant of the smooth muscle, particularly of the blood vessels and the uterus, and produce adrenergic blockade (chiefly of the alpha receptors). Used for the relief of migrain.

Physostigma is the dried seed of *Physostigma venenosum* (family Leguminosae), a vine of western Africa. It contains the alkaloid physostigimine.

Physostigmine (Eserine) is a reversible inhibitor of the cholinesterase and prevents destruction of acetylecholine. It is used as a cholinergic agent, and experimentally to enhance the action of acetylecholine at any of its sites of liberation.

Physostigimine salicylate is used by conjunctival instillation to reduce intraocular tension in glaucoma and also in the treatment of postoperative atony and urinary retension, in the management of myasthenia gravis and to counteract excessive doses of tubocurarine. P. Sulphate. Tubocurarine is an alkaloid obtained from the stems of the genus *chondodendron,* particularly *C. tomentosum.*

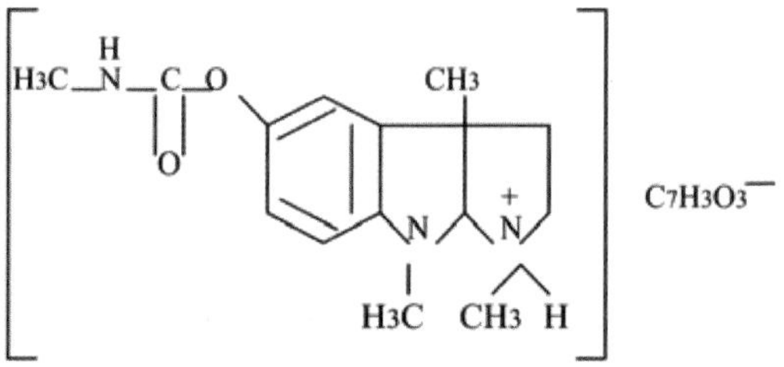

Physostigmine salicylate

ISOPRENOIDS

The isoprenoids are vast variety of biomolecules that contain repeating five - carbon structural units known as isoprene units. They consist of *terpenes* and *steroids*. Terpenes are enormous group of m olecules that are found largely in essential oils of plants. Essentials oils are plant extracts used for thousands of years in perfumes and medicines. Several thousand different types of m olecules from very different plant groups have been isolated and characterized.

Terpenes are enormous group of molecules classified according to the number of isoterpene residues they contain.

a. **Monoterpenes** are composed of t wo isorprene units. *Geraniol* is a monoterpene found in oil of geranium.

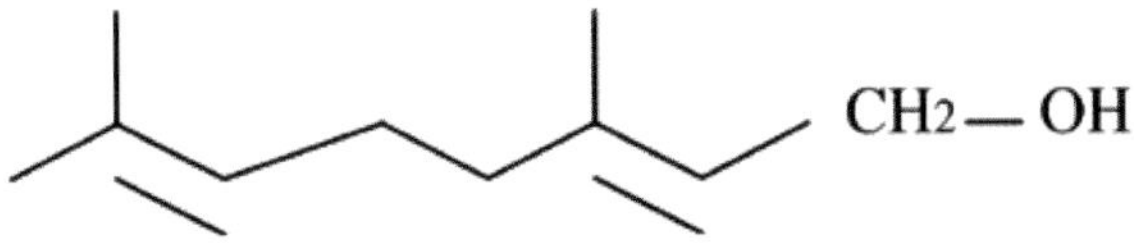

Geraniol

b. **Sesquiterpenes** contain three isoprenes. The oil of *Citronella* (used in soap and perfumes) contain the sesquiterpene *Farnesene.*

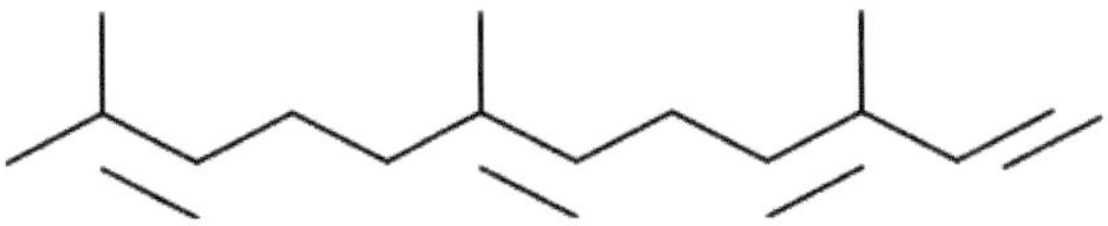

Farnesene

c. **Diterpenes** are molecules composed of four i soprene units. Phytol, a plant alcohol is the example. It is an unsaturated primary alcohol derived from the hydrolysis of chlorophyll used for the synthesis of Vitamine E and K.

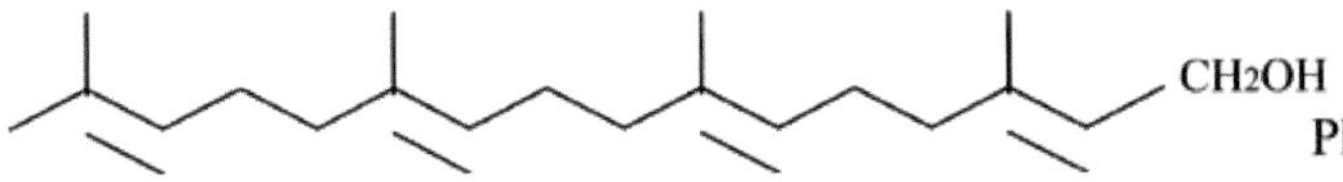

Phytol

d. **Triterpenes** contain six isoprene units. Squalene, which is found in large quantities in shark liver oil as well as olive oil and yeast, is a prominent example of triterpenes. Suqalene is an intermediate in the synthesis of steroids.

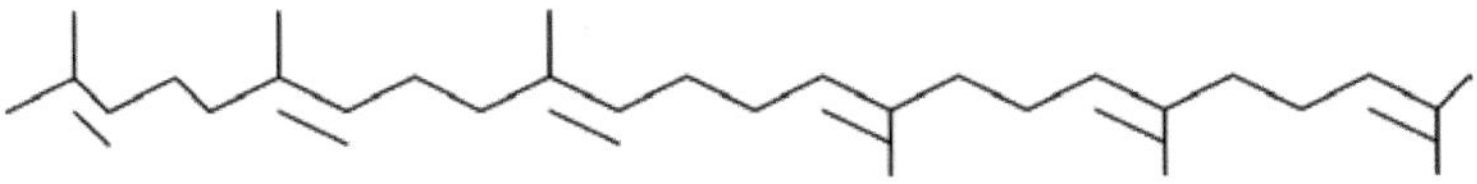

Squalene

e. **Tetraterpenes** molecules contain eight isoprene units. *Carotenoids,* the orange-colored pigments found i n most plants, are the only tetraterpenes. The carotenes are hydrocarbon members of this group. *Xanthophylls* are oxygenated derivatives of the carotenes .

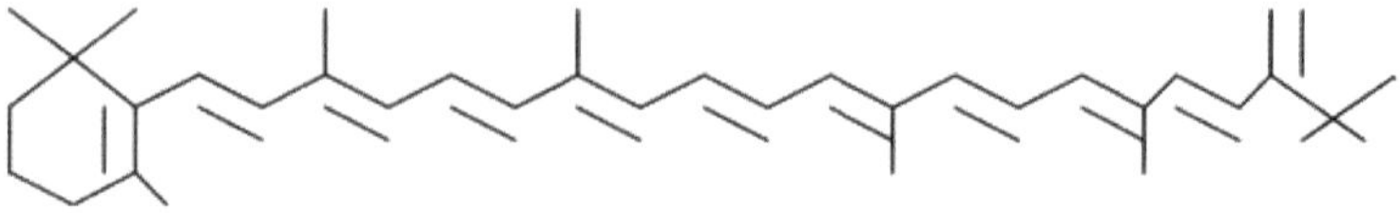

β-Carotene

f. **Polyterpenes** are high molecular weight molecules composed of hundreds or t housands of i soprene units. Natural rubber is a polyteropene composed of between 3000 and 6000 isoterpene units.

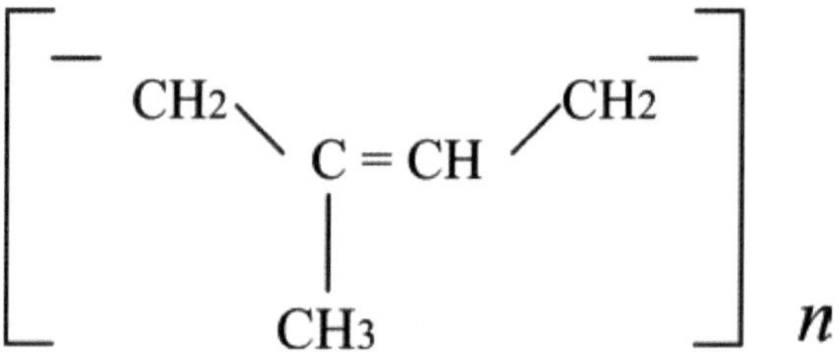

The starting product of these entire different groups is Mevalonic acid that is transformed into a phosphorylated isoprene upon phosphorylations. This isoprene polymerises subsequently. All green plants are able to generate linear isoprenoids in this way.

While terpenes with more than five isoprene units are quite universal, many of the simpler terpenes are restricted to certain plant groups. Sesquiterpene, for example, are common in mosses but occur in higher plants, too. They can be found with *Magnoliales* but not with *Ranunculales*. Gibberlins, the diterpenes are a group of phytohormones.

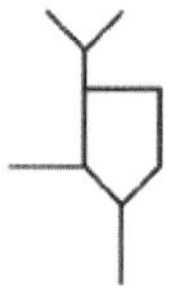

Irididane skeleton
Basic unit of the monoterpenes

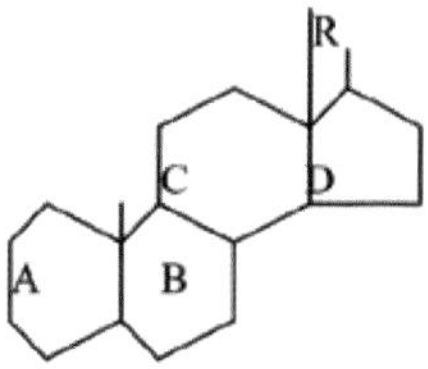

Sterane skeleton
Basic unit of a steroid.

Steroids are triterpenes or tetraterpeoids. They are found in all eukaryotes and a small number of bacteria. Each type of steroid is composed of four fus ed rings marked ABCD that have a number of additional residues – R. It is of some importance whether two of these are in a Cis -Trans position.

Steroids have been shown to occur both in gymnosperms and angiosperms. Practically all plant steroid molecules are sterols. They play an important role in membrane structure and function. The most abundant sterols in green algae and higher plants are β – sitosterol and stigmasterol.

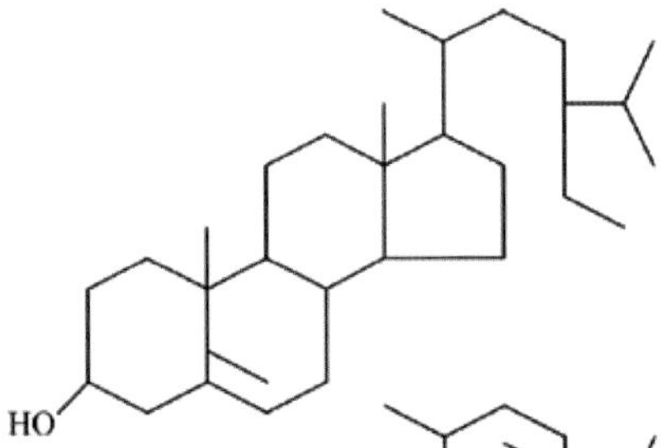

β -Sitosterol

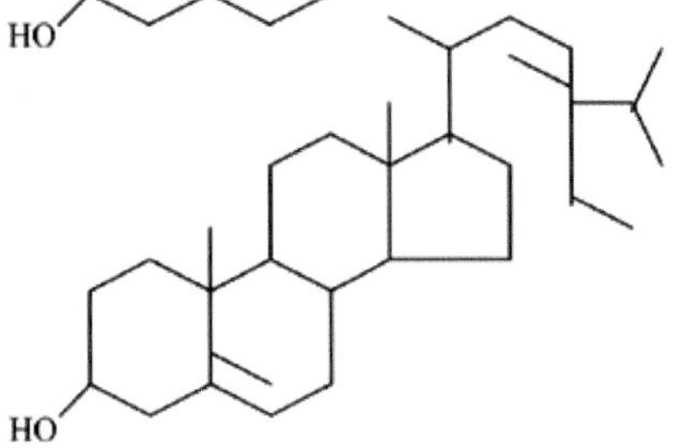

Stigmasterol

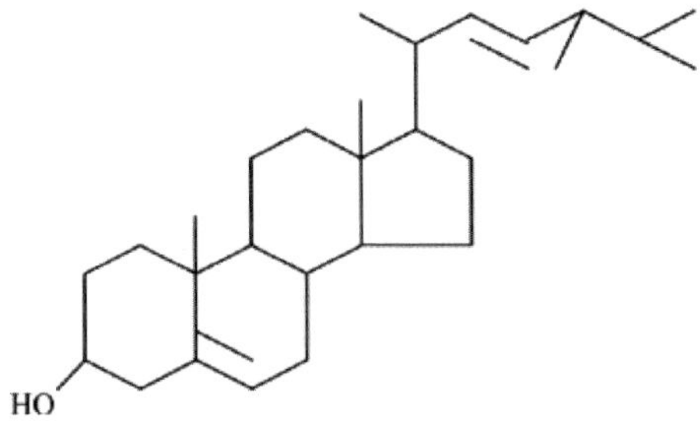

Ergasterol (found in fungi)

Cardiac glycosides are among the most interesting steroid derivatives. Several cardiac glycosides are extremely toxic. *Ouabain,* obtained from the seeds of the plant *Strophanthus gratus*, an African arrow poison or from the wood of *Acocanthera ouabaio* is poisonous while others like *digitalis*, an extract of the dried leaves of *Digitalis purpura* (the foxglove plant) is a stimulator of cardiac muscle contraction. It is used in the treatment of congestive cardiac failure.

POLYKETIDES

$CH3 - (CO - CH2)n - COOH$

Polyketides are common in Fungi and higher plants. They are secondary metabolites from bacteria, fungi, plants and animals. Secondary metabolites are organic compounds that are not directly involved in the normal growth, development or reproduction of organisms. Unlike primary metabolites, absence of secondary metabolites results not in the immediate death, but in long -term impairment of t he organism's survivability, fecundity or aesthetics, or may perhaps result in no significant change at all. Secondary metabolites are often restricted to a narrowset of species within phylogenetic group.

The function or importance of these compounds to the organism is usually of an ecological nature as they are used as defenses against predators, parasites and diseases, for interspecies competition, and to facilitate the reproductive processes (coloring agents, attractive smells, etc.). Since these compounds are usually restricted to a much more limited group of organisms, they have long been of prime importance in taxonomic research.

Polyketides are structurally a very diverse family of natural products with an extremely broad range of biological activities and pharmacological properties. Polyketide antibiotics, antifungals, cutostatics, anticholesterolemics, antiparasitics, coccidiostatics, animal growth promotants and natural insecticides are in commercial use.

Living organisms may be divided into five kingdoms. 1. Monera (Protozoan, organisms having no nucleus. 2. Protista (The lowest orders of the animal and vegetable kingdom, the protozoa and the protophyta) 3. Fungi. 4. Plants and 5. Animals. Fungi and plants are source of Medicines.

Since the discovery of antibiotic properties ofpolyketides (i.e., Streptomycine in 1950), the research of new compounds had led pharmaceutical companies to isolate tens of millions of anitibiotic producing strains through cultivabe soil microorganisms and other active compounds. (Zaehner and Fieldler,1995; Charusanti et al.,2012)

Polyketides are derived from the polymerization of acetyl and propionyl sub-units in a similar process to fatty acid synthesis .

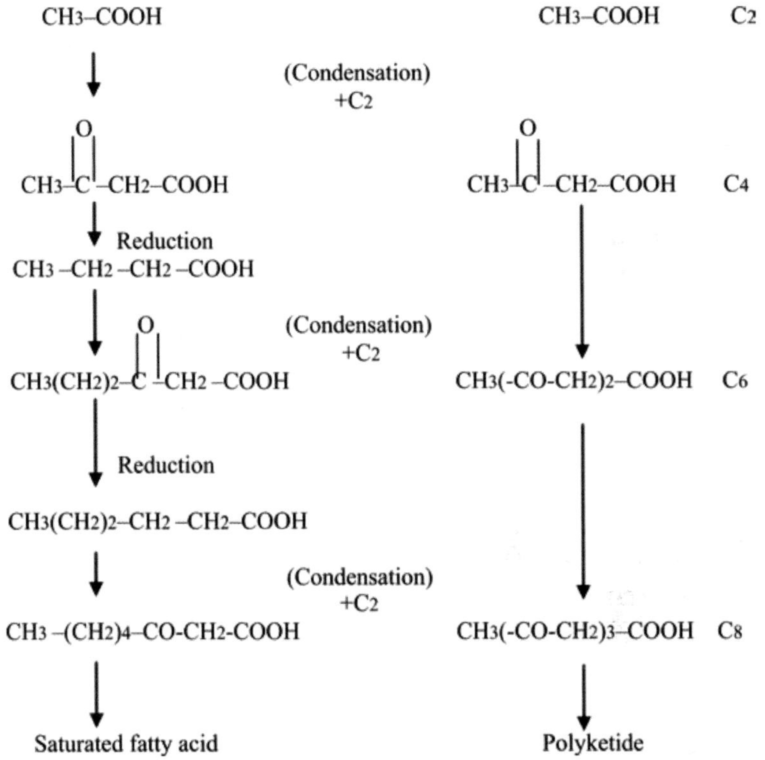

There is a close parallel between the biosynthesis of fa tty acids and poly-ketides, since in both cases, the formation of l inear chains proceeds by an addition of C2 units. The difference is that in fatty acid biosynthesis every C2 unit is added to the growing chain only after the reduction of t he previous carbonyle unit to a methylene group; but the growth of the polyketide chain does not usually require such a prior reduction. Instead poly- beta-ketoacids are formed. Such compounds are very reactive since they contain both active methylene groups (Potential nucleophiles) and carbonyl groups (potential electrophiles)

Among the secondary metabolites produced mainly by the higher plants and macro organisms, anthracyclines and polyketide antibiotics synthesized by *Streptomyces* species are of particular medical importance. Anthracyclines are clinically most potent anti-tumor drugs.

Sources of Secondary metabolites

Higher plants

ANTHRACENE DERIVATIVES

Eg.

Senna (dried leaflets of *Cassia acutifolia –Alexandrine Sp.)*

C. angustifolia –Tinnevelly or Indian Sp

Family: leguminosae

Cascara (Cascara sagrada. Dired bark of *Rhamnus purshiana)*

Family: Rhamnaceae

C. amarga –Family: Simarubaceae

Rhubarb (any plant of the genus *Rheum)*

Rhubarb officinale, R. palmatum

Family: Polygonaceae

Fungi

TETRACYCLINES

ERYTHROMYCINE

GRISEOFULVIN

(all are antibiotics)

Aloe (dried juice from the leaves of plants of the genus *Aloe*

Aloe perryi, A. barbadensis, A. ferox, A. Africana, A. spicata

A number of glycosides with aglycones related to *Anthracene* are present in drugs such as

- Senna
- Cascara sagrada
- Rhubarb
- Aloe.

ANTHRACENE

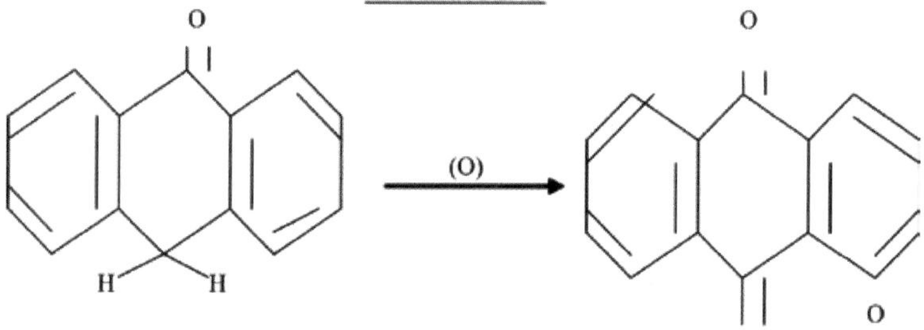

Anthrones

Anthroquinone (oxidized derivative

These drugs are employed as cathartics. The glycosides, upon hydrolysis, yield aglycones that are di-tri-or tetra hydroxy anthroquinone or modifications of these compounds.

The free anthroquinone aglycones exhibit little therapeutic activity. The sugar residue facilitates absorption and translocation of the aglycone to the site of action. The anthroquinone and related glycosides are stimulant cathartics and exert their action by increasing the tone of the smooth muscle in the wall of the large intestine.

Glycosides of anthranols and anthrocene elicit a more drastic action than do the corresponding anthraquinone glycosides.

SENNA

Cassia acutifolia – Alexandrine Sp.

C. angustifolia – Tinnevelly or Indian Sp.

Family*: LEGUMINOSAE*

The leaves are used in making tablets. The pod, besides crushed to make tablets is most commonly used for preparation of Senna infusion (tea). The active principle constituents of Senna are dimeric glycosides called Sennosides A, B, C, and D. The aglycones are composed of the aloe -emodin + rhein for A and B and rhein + rhein for C and D.

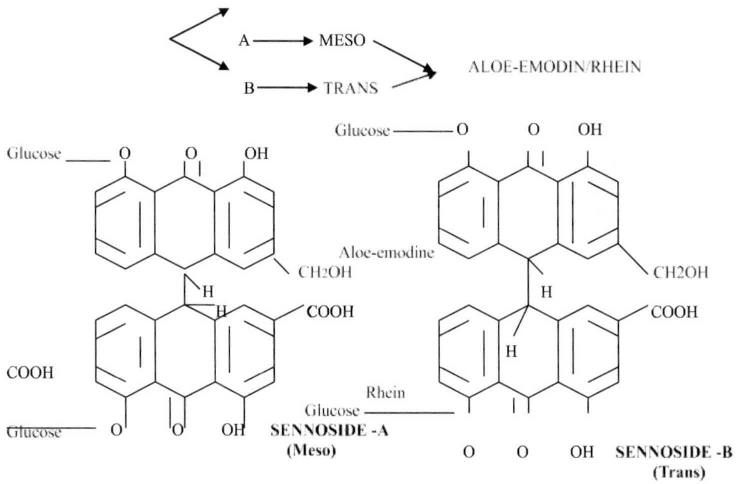

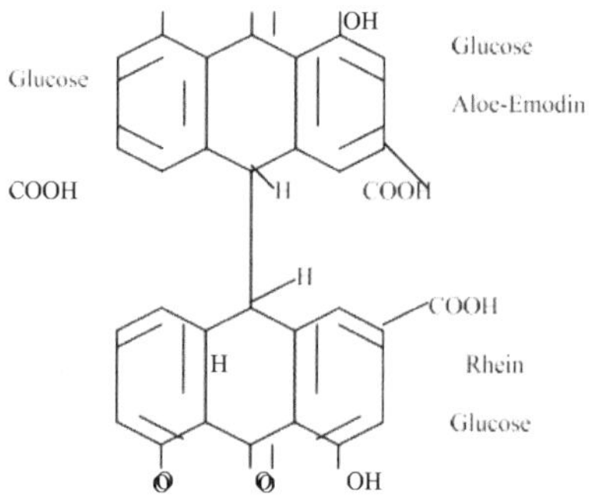

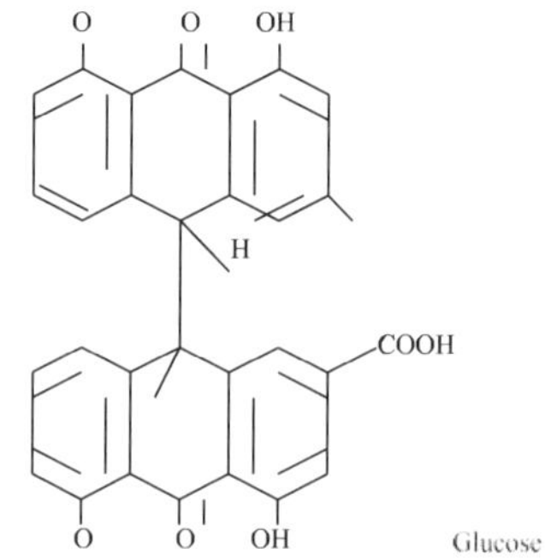

SENNOSIDE C (MESO) SENNOSIDE D (TRANS)

The sennosides are water-soluble but the meso form is more soluble than the transform. All the four glycosides are responsible for the activity of Senna.

PHARMACOLOGY: The anthraquinon glycosides pass unchanged into the colon where bacteria hydrolyse the glycoside bond yielding the free anthraquinone, which has a direct stimulant effect on the myentric plexus, resulting in smooth muscle activity and thus defecation.

Some of the drug is also absorbed and excreted in the urine and may appear in breast milk. There is evidence to suggest that long continued use of anthroquinone purgatives result in damage to the myentric plexus. Long term use or misuse can result in dependency and electrolyte loss. Senna should not be used during pregnancy or lactation.

FLAVONOIDS

Flavonoids constitute one of the most characteristic classes of compounds in higher plants. Many flavonoids are easily recognized as flower pigments in most angiosperm families (flowering plants). However, their occurrence is not restricted to flowers but include all parts of the plant. They have been referred to as "nature's biological response modifiers" because of strong experimental evidence of their inherent ability to modify the body's reaction to allergens, viruses, and carcinogens. They show anti-allergic, anti- inflammatory, anti-microbial and anti-cancer activity.

The flavonoids are polyphenolic compounds possessing 15 carbon atoms; two benzine rings joined by a linear three carbon chain, represented below as the C6-C3-C6 system.

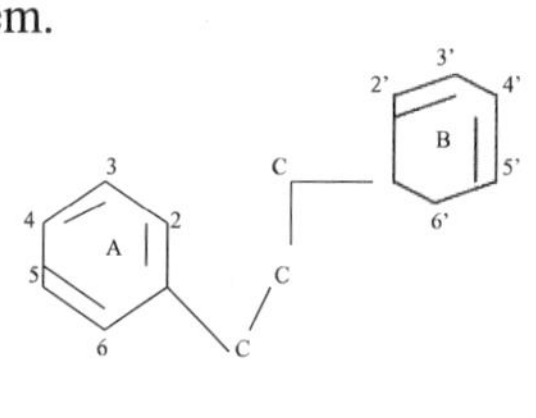

The chemical structure of the flavonoids are based on a C15 skeleton with Cromane ring bearing a second aromatic ring B in position 2,3 or 4

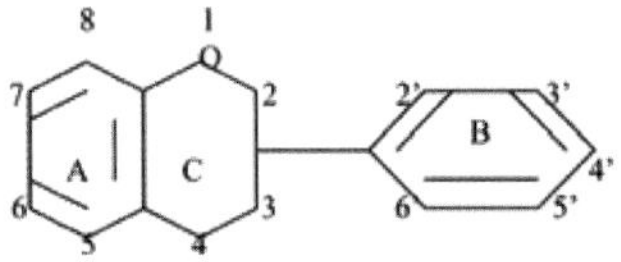

In a few cases, the six-numbered heterocyclic ring 'C' occurs in an isomeric open form or in replaced, by a five-numbered ring

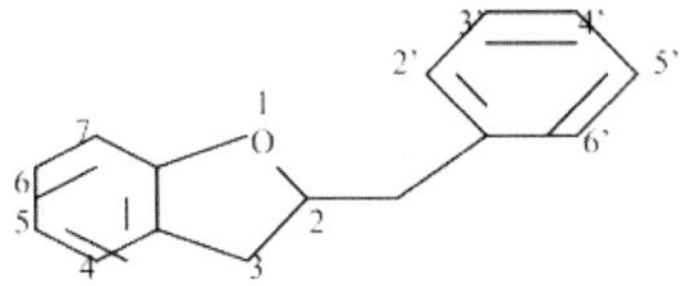

The oxygen bridge involving the central carbon atom (C2) of the 3C – chain occurs in a rather limited number of cases, where the resulting heterocyclic is of the FURAN type. Various such groups of flavonoids are classified according to the substitute pattern of ring C. Both the oxidation state of the heterocyclic ring and the position of ring B are important as the classification.

Examples of the 6 major subgroups are:

1. **CHALCONE**

3-phenylacrylephenone; benzylidene acetophenone, is the parent compound of a series of plant pigments.

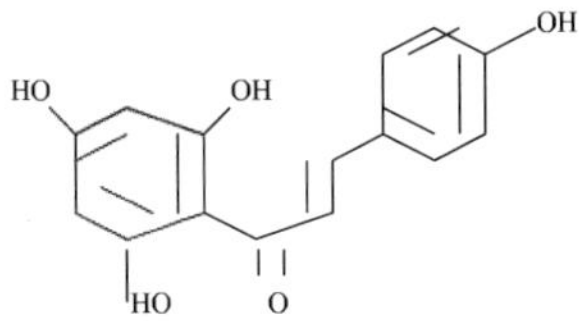

2. **FLAVONE**

Generally in herbaceous families; Eg. *Labiatae, Umbelliferae, Compositae*)

Apigenin (*Apiumgraveolense, Petroselinum srispum*)
Luteolin (*Equisetumarvense*)

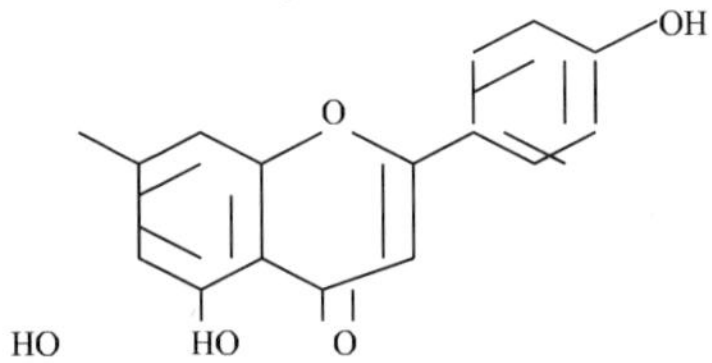

3. FLAVONOL

Generally in woody angiosperms

Quercitol (*Ruta graveolens, Fagopyrum esculentum, Sambucus nigra*)

Kaempferol (*Sambucus nigra, Cassia Senna, Equisetrum arvense, Lamiumalbam, Polygonum bistorta*)

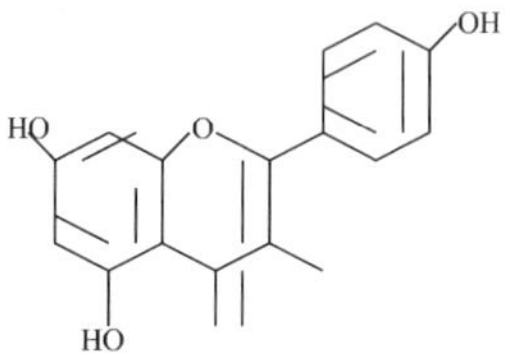

4. FLAVONONE

Is 2,3-Dihydroflavone

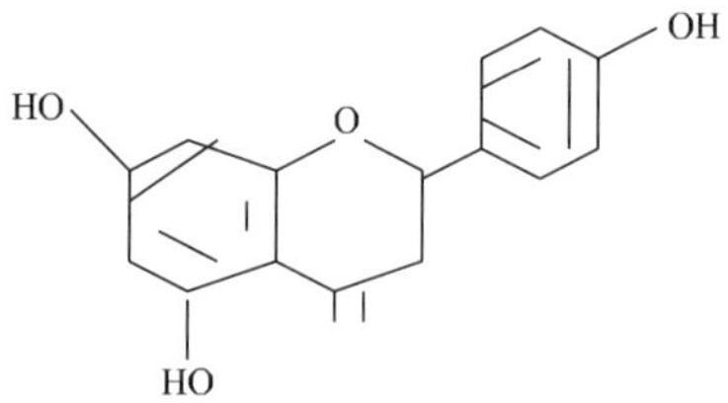

5. ANTHOCYANINS

Anthocyanins are a group of floral pigments, ranging from red to blue. They are soluble in water and alcohol and not in ether.

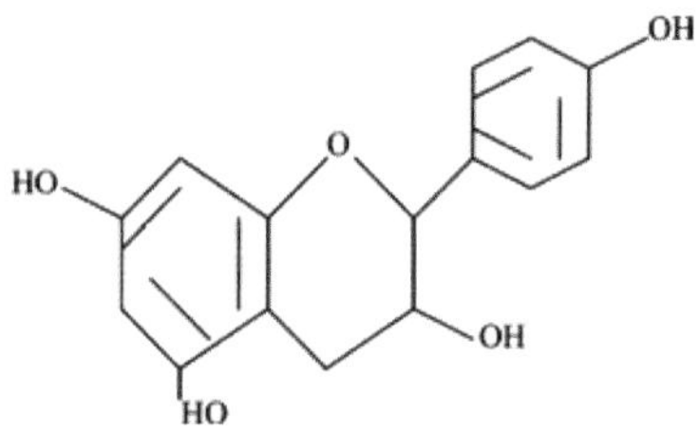

6. ISOFLAVONOIDS

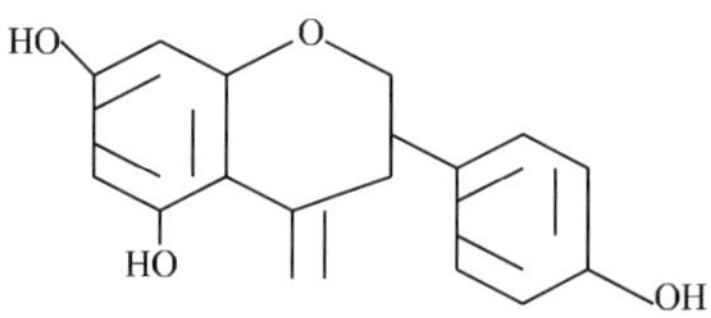

Most of these (flavonones, flavones, flavonoids and anthocyanins) bear ring B in position 2 of t he heterocyclic ring. In i soflavonoids, ring B oc cupies position 3.

Types of Flavonoids

- ➢ Chalcone
- ➢ Anthocyanidin
- ➢ Isoflavonoides
- ➢ Rotenone
- ➢ Neoflavanoids
- ➢ Flavanolignans

Chalcone

Chalcones are intermediate in the biosynthesis of flavonoids, which are substances wide spread in the plants and with an array of b iological activities. They show antibacterial, anti fungal, anti tumour and anti inflammatory properties.

Chalcone is derived from three acetate and cinnamic acid
as shown below.

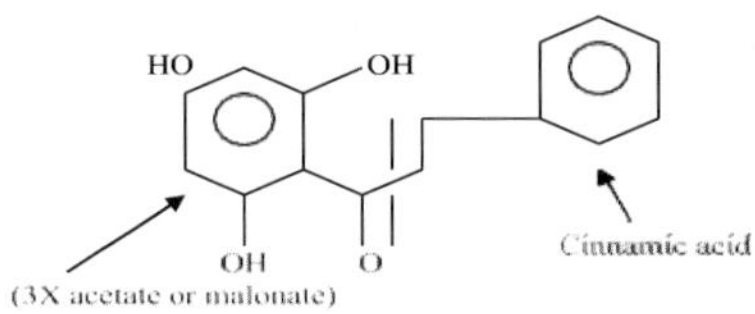

Anthocyanidin

The anthocyanidins constitute a large family of differently colored compounds and occur in countless mixtures in practically all parts of hi gher plants. They are of gre at economic importance as fruit pigments and so are used to color fruit juices, wine and some beverages.

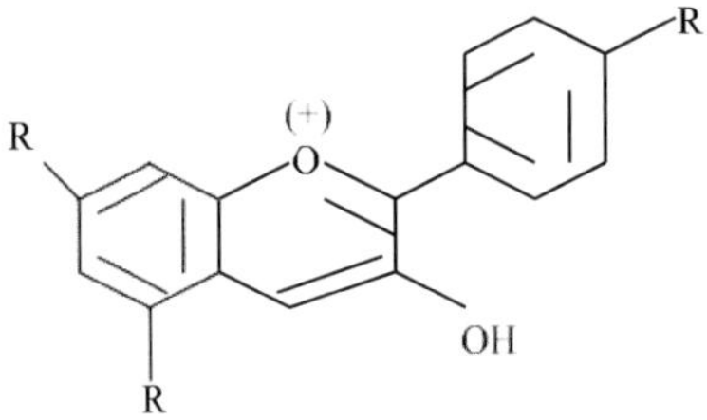

Anthocyanidin is an extended conjugate made up of the aglycone of the glycoside anthocyanines. Next to the chlorophylls anthocyanines are the most important group of plant pigments visible to human eyes.

GLYCOSIDES	=	AGLYCONE	+	GLYCENE
↓		↓		↓
ANTHOCYANIN		ANTHOCYANIDIN		SUGAR

In December 2004 a peer-reviewed study at Michigan State University published by the American Chemical Society noted that anthocyanin could boost insulin production by up to 50%. However the study leader noted that despite the initial excitement, more study would be needed. Also in 2005, an article published in Applied and Environmental Microbiology demonstrated for the first time the biosynthesis of anthocyanins in bacteria. In 2007 a study at the University of Pittsburgh discovered that anthocyanins kill human cancer cells while not affecting healthy cells. At low doses of cyanidine-3-rutinoside (C-3 -R), half of the cancer cells in all lines of the test human leukemia and lymphoma cells died within 18 hours. When the amount of C-3-R was more than doubled, all of the cancer cells died within 18 hours. The mechanism seems to be that cancerous cells respond to C-3-R by releasing peroxides which kills the cells. Normal cells do not release peroxides when C-3-R is administered. Dr. Xiao-Ming Yin, an associate professor of pathology at the University of 'Pittsburg School of Medicines' said "the hope is that black raspberries and other botanicals might provide doctors with less toxic alternative drug and radiation therapy.

The anthocyanidin in Hydrangea, colors it *red* in acid soil and *blue* in alkali soil.

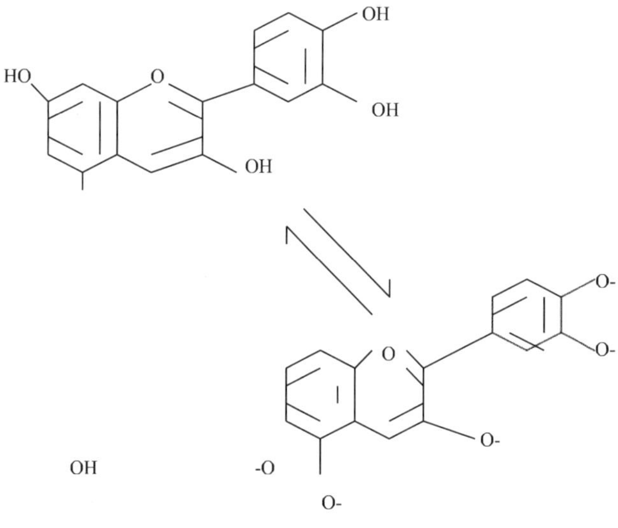

They will chelate with metal ions like Ca 2+ and Mg 2+ under alkali conditions.
This extends the conjugation as shown below.

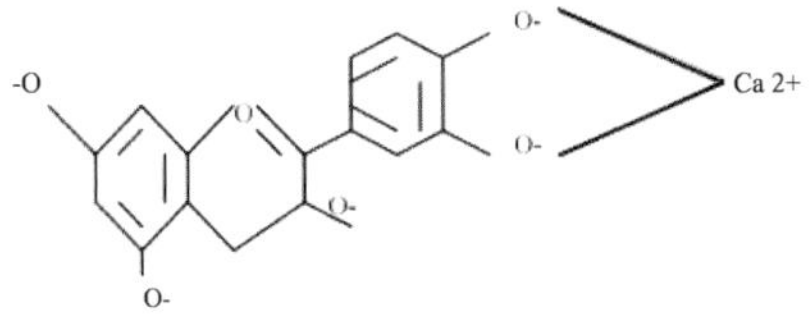

Isoflavonoids

The isoflavonoids are all colourless. In c ontrast to most other flavonoids, isoflavonoids have a rather limited taxonomic distribution, mainly within the *Leguminosae.*

It has been established that acetate gives rise to ring A and that Phenylalamine Cinnamate and Cinnamate derivatives are incorporated in to ring B and C –2,-3, and –4 of the heterocyclic ring.

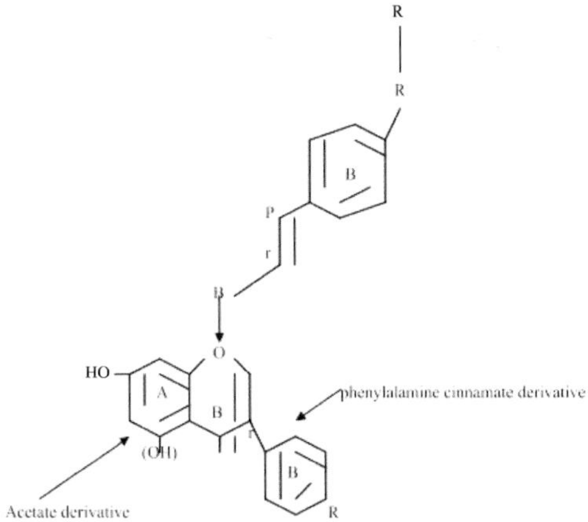

Chalones and flavonones are efficient precursors of i soflavanoids. Recently, soy isoflavonoids have been subject to much medical attention. Studies indicate that they have a variety of beneficial health effects based on the fact that the molecular structure of the isoflavonoids is very similar to the body´s own oestrogen. The isoflavonoids thus help to balance oestrogen levels in the body, reducing the hormone-related complaints associated with menopause. Research also suggests that the isoflavonoids are beneficial for cardiovascular health.

Rotenone

Rotenone is a biologically active isoflavonoid. It is a component of derris root -*Derris elliptica, D. malaccensis* and *Lonchocarpus nicou* (*Family: Leguminosae*) used externally for the treatment of scabies and infestation with chiggers and in veterinary medicine for follicular management and infestation with lice, fleas and ticks. It is also used as insecticide and is a fish poison.

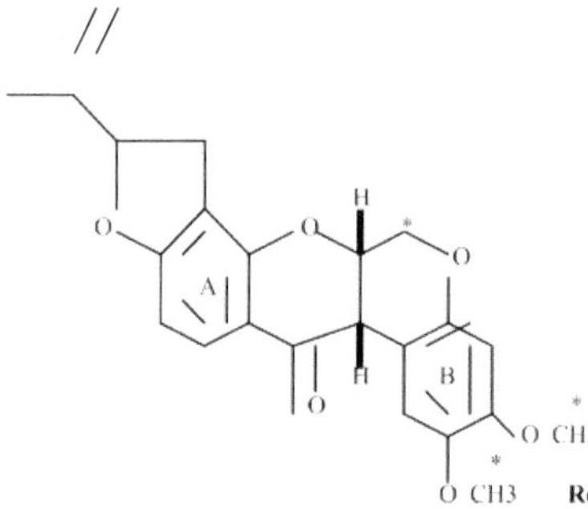

Rotenone

Rotenone is most potent. It is unstable in light and heat and almost all toxicity can be lost after two to three days during summer. It is very toxic to fish, one of its main uses by native people, over the centuries being to paralyze fish for capture and consumption. Crystalline rotenone has an acute oral lethal dose (LD) 50 of 60 , 132 and 3000 mg/kg for guinea pigs, rats, and rabbits (Matsumura 1,985). Because the toxicity of derris powders exceeds that of the equivalent content of rotenone, it is obvious that the other esters in crude preparations have significant biologic activity.

Acute poisoning in animals is characterized by an initial respiratory stimulation followed by respiratory depression, ataxia, convulsions and death by respiratory arrest (Shirukin and Aderson, 1936). The anaesthetic like action on nerves appears to be related to the ability of rotenone to block electron transport in mitochondria by inhibiting oxidation linked NADH2, this resulting in nerve conduction blockade (O'Brien 1967; Corbet, 1974). The estimated fatal oral dose for a 70 Kg man is of the order of 10 –100gm. Rotenone has been used topically for treatment of head lice, scabies, and other ecto-parasites, but the dust is highly irritating to the eyes (Conjunctivitis), the skin (dermatitis), and to the upper respiratory tracts (rhinitis) and throat (pharyngitis).

Neoflavonoids

Flavonoids in which ring B is attached to C-4 or as 4-phenylcoumarins are called as neoflavonoid. Two neoflavonoid compounds, *Dalbergione* I and II related to *Obtusastyrene* (4-cinnamylphenol) isolated from *Dalbergis nigra* were found to be effect antimicrobials against gram positive and negative bacteria and acid fast bacteria and some fungi.

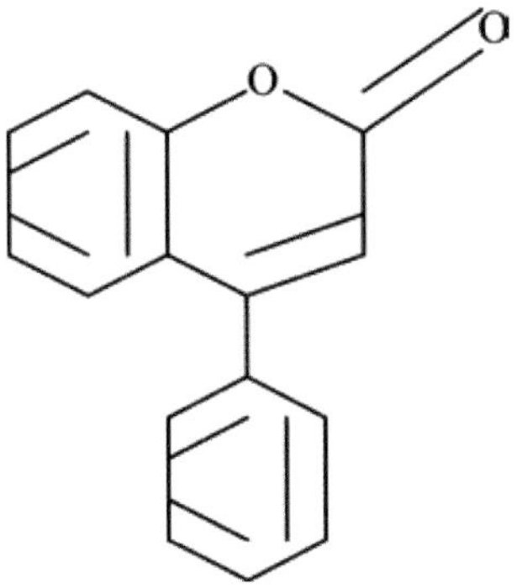

Neoflavonoid base

The isoflavonoid and neoflavonoids are graded as abnormal flavonoids.

Flavanolignans

Flavanolignans are flavonoids bound to lignanas. *Silymarin* is the collective name for t he flavonolignans extracted from milk thistle, including *silybin, silydianin, and silychristin.* Silybin is the most biologically active substance. Flavonolignans represent natural compounds whose biosynthesis presumes a radical coupling of a ring B catecholic flavonoid with a molecule of coniferyl alcohol or an analogue. Many natural flavonolignans can exist as regioisomers, depending on how the coupled coniferyl alcohol moiety orients to the flavonoid.

Milk Thistle has been used traditionally for the treatment of liver and gall blader disorders. The terms "milk thistle" and "silymarin" are often used interchangeably.

A number of other flavonolignans have been reported in the seeds including dehydrosilybin, desoxysilycristin, desoxysilydianin, silandrin, silybinome, silyhermin, and neosilyhermin. In addition apigenin, silybonol, and myristic, palmitic, stearic, and oleic acids have been described, as well as betaine, known as a hepatoprotector, and essential fatty acids, which reportedly contribute to silymarin's anti-inflammatory effect.

Currently the primary medical application of milk thistle is its use as a hepatoprotectant and as supportive treatment of chronic inflammatory liver disorders such as cirrhosis, hepatitis, and fatty infiltration due to alcohol and toxic chemicals. It has also been used in the treatment of liver damage by poisonous mushrooms.

LIGNANS

(*Sesame oil, Pyrethrum, Podophyllotoxin, Etoposide*)

The lignans comprise a class of natural plant products which are derived from Cinnamic acid derivative and which are related bio-chemically to phenylalanine metabolism. They fall into five major such groups and the nomenclature in use is neither consistent between the groups nor even within the subgroups. Many lignans show physiological activity such as the tumor inhibiting podophyllotoxin. This specific activity leads to interference with cell division by two different mechanisms, in animals including humans. Some are active in suppressing the CNS and inhibiting the cyclic AMP phospodiesterase, while others act as fish poisoning or germination inhibitors. In Chinese traditional medicine lignans are used for the treatment of viral hepatitis, and protection of the liver.

Properties: Anti cancerous, prevents heart diseases and also used in menopausal syndromes.

Basically, lignans are considered to act as plant hormones. When bacteria in the digestive tract act on plant lignans, these compounds are converted into potent, hormone like substances known as phytoestrogenic compound.

The promising evidence surrounding the dietary benefits of consuming foods with high lignan content revolves around the low incidence of breast, colon and prostate cancers found with those people who regularly eat food with high lignan content. Research findings are concluding that the chemical re- lease of these plant hormones in the body, are able to block the action of c ertain cancer causing substances.

Researchers believe these plant hormones mimic the body's own estrogen type of cells and can block the formation of hormone based tumors or growth. Unlike the hormones produced in the body these plant hormones do not stimulate cancerous cells to grow. In fact, lignans boost production of a substance that fastens in to human estrogen and carries it out of the body. They are also considered to be anti-oxidants, therefore, researchers believe lignans can protect healthy cells from cancer causing agents (known as free radicals).

Lignans and isoflavonoids are abundant in plasma of subjects living areas with low cancer incidence and are often referred to as Phenolic Phytoprotectants (the so called PPS). Lignans and isoflavonoid glycosides are converted by bacteria in the intestine to hormone like substances, which influence malignant cell proliferation and other factors in such a way as to make them strong candidates as natural cancer-protective agents.

Lignans are also believed to be a protective barrier against heart diseases and menopausal symptoms.

Source: Lignans are present in cereals, grains, nuts, fruits, vegetables, pumpkin seeds whole grains, cram berries, fresh broccoli, whole wheat bread, black or green tea. But FLAX SEED is certainly considered to be the storehouse of lignans and is more in the matrix of the seed. Cooking flax seed apparently does not decrease the amount of lignans absorbed by the body; however it may damage another healthful flax seed constituent, the essential fatty acid – alpha-linoleic acid (ALA).

Many plant food have some lignans, yet flax seed has proven to be the super food with boasting anywhere from 75 to 800 times the amount of lignan as other gram and vegetable sources.

Contraindication: Because of the potential effect on estrogen avoid taking large amounts of lignan either if you are pregnant or breast-feeding.

COUMARINS

C9H6O2

Coumarin is found in high percentages in the tonka bean (*Dipteryx odorata, Family: Fabaceae*). Many other plants like cinnamon, lavender, woodruff, sweet clover; strawberries, apricots, cherries, and oils of Fennel, Bergamot, Sage, Chamommille and citrus oils also are common sources.

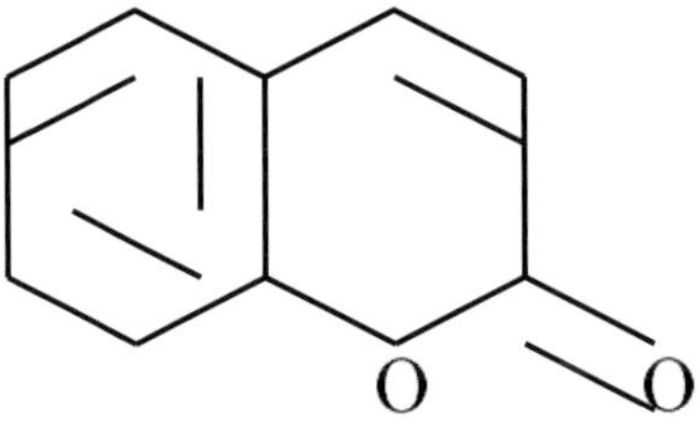

Coumarin

Coumarin has a sweet scent, readily recognised as the scent of newly -mown hay and is used as a natural flavouring and perfume. It has clinical value as the precursor for several anticoagulants notably warfarin. It is also used as a gain medium in some dye lasers.

Some naturally occurring coumarin derivatives include umbelliferone (7-hydroxycoumarin), Aesculetin (6,7-dihydroxycoumarin), Scopoletin, Psoralen and Imperatorin. Coumarin and its derivatives are all considered phenylpropanoids.

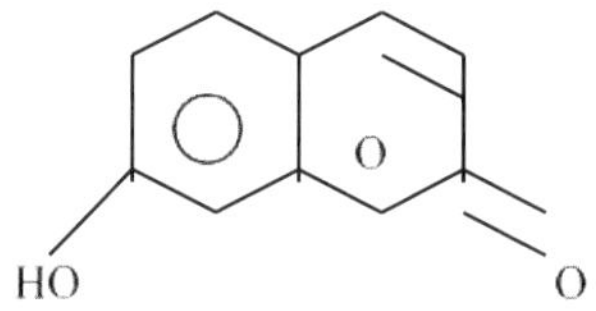

Umbellitrone

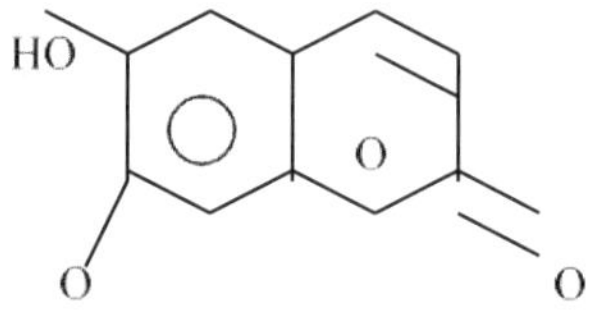

Ausculetin

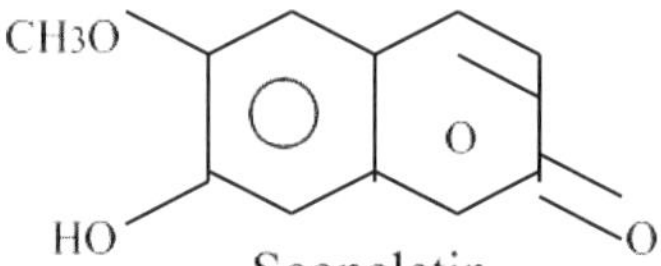

Scopeletin

Umbelliferone is obtained from the gum resin of many plants of the *family Umbelliferae*. Aesculetin is the aglucone of esculin, a glucoside from the bark of *horse-chestnut* and used as a sunburn protective. Psoralen is a phototoxic drug used in the treatment of vitiligo.

GLYCOSIDES

Glycosides are often found in nature. One example is *Salicin*, a compound found in *willow tree bark* . Conversion of salicin to salicicylic acid is one step in the production of the modern analgesic aspirin (acetylsalicylic acid).

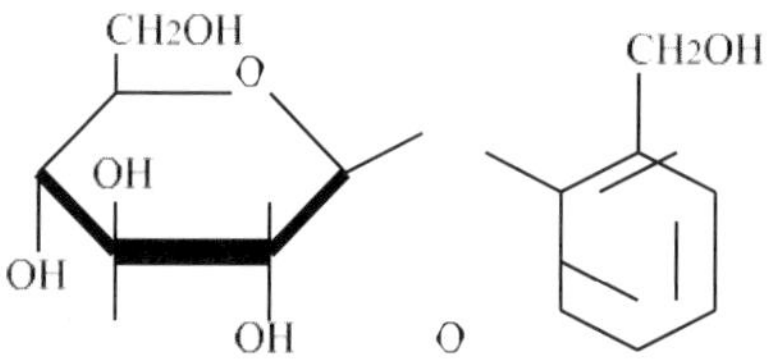

Salicin

Glycosides are compounds containing a *Carbohydrate* and a *Non-carbohydrate* residue in the same molecule. The carbohydrate residue is attached to a non-carbohydrate residue, or *aglycone* by an *acetal lionkage* at Carbon atom 1. Hemiacetals react with alcohols to form *acetal*. The new linkage is called acetal linkage or *glycoside linkage,* and the component is called a *glycoside*. The non-sugar component is known as the **aglycone.** The sugar component is called the **glycone.** The name of the glycoside specifies the sugar component. For example, acetals of glucose and fructose are called *glucosides and fructosides*, respectively.

If an acetal linkage is formed between the hemiacetal hydroxyl group of one monosaccharide and a hydroxyl group of another monosaccharide, the resulting glycoside is called a *disaccharide*. A molecule containing large number of monosaccharides linked by glycoside linkage is called a *polysaccharide*.

Based on the chemical nature of the aglycone group glycosides are classified as follows:

GLYCOSIDES

- **Tanin group**
- **Cardioactive group**
- **Aldehyde group**
- **Anthraquinone group**
- **Alcohol group**
- **Saponine group**
- **Lactone group**
- **Cyanophore group**
- **Isothiocyanate group**
- **Phenol group**
- **Flavonol group**

> Cellulose is the most important structural polysaccharide of plants. The ability to digest cellulose is found only in micro organisms that possess the enzyme cellulase. It is one of the several plant products that make up the dietary fiber that now believed to be important for good health.

Saponins

Saponins are a class of non -nitrogenous glycosides found i n many plants, which possess the common property of foaming when strongly agitated in aqueous solution; they can hold resinous and fatty substances in suspension in water. They are amorphous bodies as a rule, though a few are crystallizable, and possess the properties of glycosides. They are irritants when applied to the skin or mucous membranes, and given internally cause nausea and vomiting.

Saponin on hydrolysis gives an aglycone known as "Sapogenin"

Saponin = Sugar (*glycone*) + Sapogenin (*aglycone)*

The *neutral* saponins are derivatives of steroids with spiroketal side chains. The *acid* saponins possess triterpenoid structure.

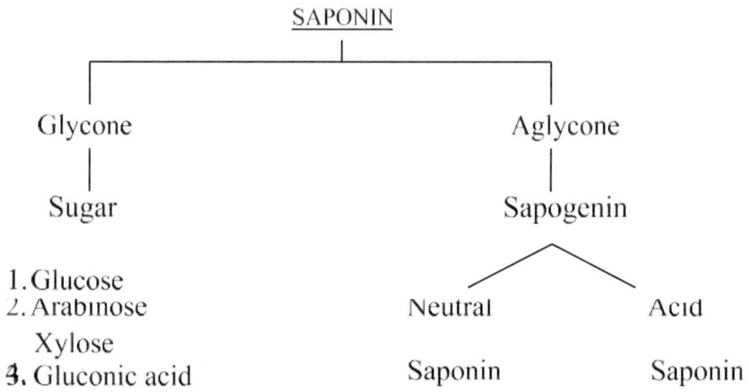

Arabinose is pectin sugar, a pentose widely distributed in plants, usually in complex polysaccharides. It is used in culture media. Xylose is wood sugar, an aldopentose isomeric with ribose. It is obtained by fermentation or hydrolysis of naturally occurring carbohydrate substances. Eg. wood fiber. Gluconic acid is the hexonic (aldonic) acid derived from glucose by oxidation.

> Saponins occur in many plant species to resist the fungal attack. But many fungi develop defence against it forming saponin detoxifying enzymes. For example *Septoria lycopersici*, a pathogen of tomato (*Solanum lycopersicum*) produces saponin detoxyfying enzyme, *Tomatinase* against defence of saponin in tomato.

LICORICE(Glycyrrhizaglabra)

Family: Leguminosae

Glycyrrhiza is the dried rhizome and roots of Glycyrrhiza glabra and allied species. It is demulcent, slightly laxative and expectorant. Glycyrrhiza contains a saponin glycoside called Glycyrrhizin.

Glycyrrhizin

Glycyrrhizin has two molecules of glucuronic acid (*glycone*) and a glycyrrhetinic acid (*aglycone*).

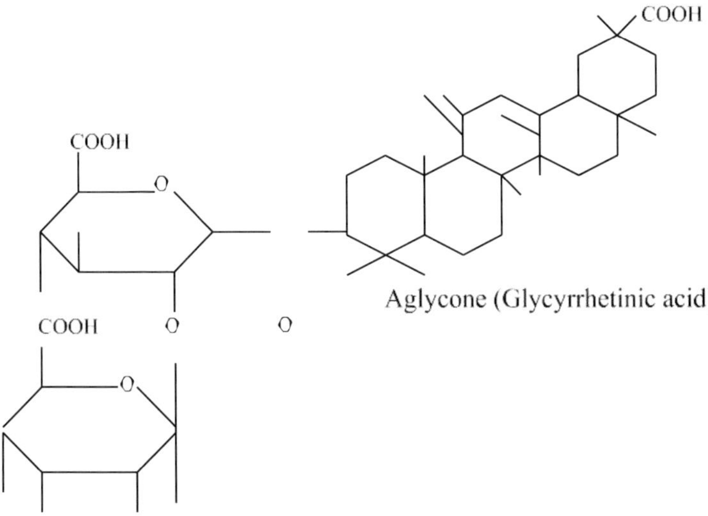

Aglycone (Glycyrrhetinic acid)

Two molecules of glycone
(Glucuronic acid)

Glycyrrhizin is the Ca 2+ and K+ salts of glycyrrhizinic acid. It is 50 times sweeter than sugar (sucrose). Upon hydrolysis, the glycoside loses its sweet taste and is converted to the aglycon glycyrrhitinic acid plus two molecules of glucuronic acid.

Glycyrrhetinic acid is a pentacyclic triterpenoid derivative of the beta - amyrine type. It has expectorant and antitussive properties. It is used considerably as a flavoring agent and is frequently employed to mask the taste of bitter drugs such as aloe, quinine etc.

In Ayurveda licorice is used to treat heart burn; mouth, gastric, duodenal and esophageal ulceration and inflammation.

Glycyrrhetinic acid inhibits the enzyme (15 – hydroxy prostaglandin dehydrogenase & delta 13 – prostaglandin) that metabolizes the prostaglandins, PGE2 and PGF 2alpha to their respective 15 Keto, 14-dihydro- metabolites, which are inactive. This causes an increased level of prostaglandins in the digestive systems. Prostaglandins inhibit gastric secretion but stimulate pancreatic secretion and mucous secretion in the intestines and markedly increase intestinal motility. They also cause cell proliferation in the stomach. The effect on gastric acid secretion, promotion of mucous secretion, and cell proliferation shows why licorice has potential in treating peptic ulcer.

PGF2alpha stimulates activity of the uterus during pregnancy and cause abortion; therefore licorice should not be taken during pregnancy.

In the past, individuals who had undiagnosed Addison's disease found that consumption of large amount of licorice provided some relief from their symptoms. In these patients, licorice consumption resulted in sodium retention, hypokalemia and a rise in blood pressure. This effect was more pronounced when cortisol was administered. Recently, it has been discovered that the active ingredient in licorice, the glycyrrhizic acid, inhibits 11 – β-hydroxysteriod dehydrogenase, the enzyme that reversibly converts cortisol to cortisone, its active metabolite.

The structure of the glycyrrhetinic acid is similar to that of cortisone. Both nucleus are flat and similar at position 3 and 11. This might be the basis for licorice's anti-inflammatory action.

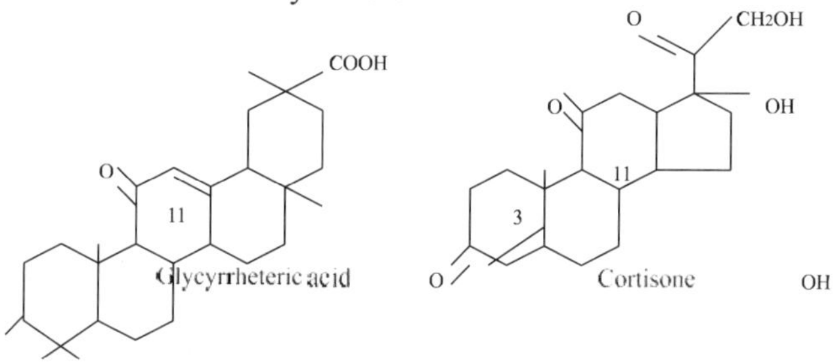

Glycyrrhizin inhibits liver cell injury caused by many chemicals and is used in the treatment of chronic hepatitis and cirrhosis in Japan. It also inhibits the growth of several DNA and RNA viruses, inactivating herpes simplex particles irreversibly.

- Licorice should not be given to patients with a known history of high blood pressure
- Prolonged use of licorice can also cause the formation of cataracts.
- Also it should not be given in pregnancy.

CARDIAC GLYCOSIDES

Remember that glycosides are carbohydrate containing - acetals. Cardiac glycosides are most interesting steroid derivatives. Several, like *ouabain,* obtained from the seeds of the plant *Strophanthus gratus* are extremely toxic while others like *digitalis,* an extract of the dried leaves of *Digitalis pupurea* have valuable medicinal properties.

In ouabain the glycone is one one rhamnose residue. The steroid aglycone of ouabain is called *ouabagenin*

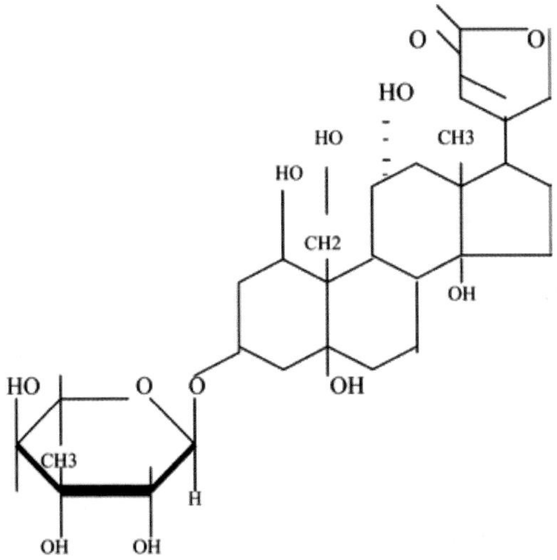

Ouabain glycoside

Digitalis

Digitonin is a Digitalis drug derived from *Digitalis purpurea.* It is used in modern medicine to increase the force of the systolic contractions and prolong duration of the diastolic phase in congestive heart failure. Digitalis drugs lower venous pressure in hypersensitive heart ailments, elevate blood pressure in a weak heart, act as a diuretic, and reduce edema. However, the therapeutic dose is dangerously close to the lethal dose.

Historically, Foxglove was employed by herbalists for a variety of purposes, from an ointment used for cleansing wounds and reducing swelling to boiling it and using it as an expectorant.

Hydrolysis of digitalis produces three major aglycones or genins, all which contain alpha, beta-unsaturated lactone ring (cyclic ester) in addition to other structural similarities. Both the C_{14} (beta) hydroxyl group and the unsaturated lactone are essential to its activity as a drug.

1. Gitoxgenin

2. Digitoxygenin

3. Digoxigenin

Gitoxigenin

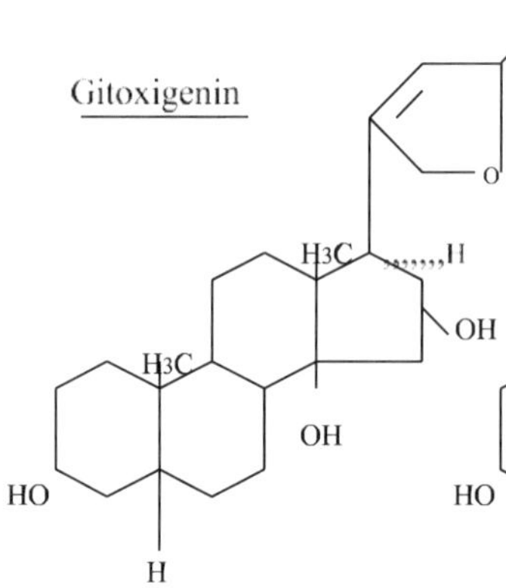

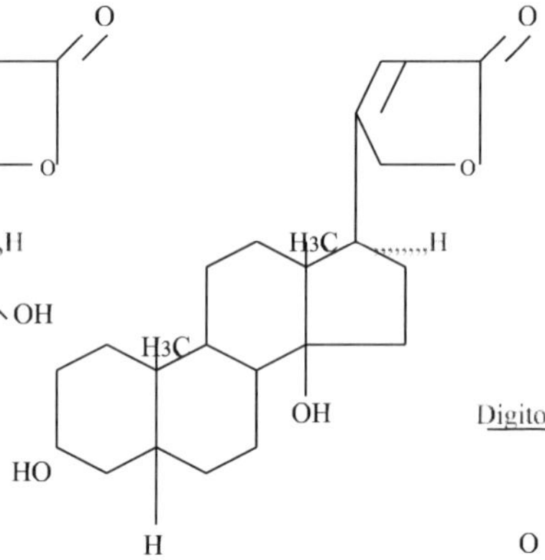

Digitoxygenin

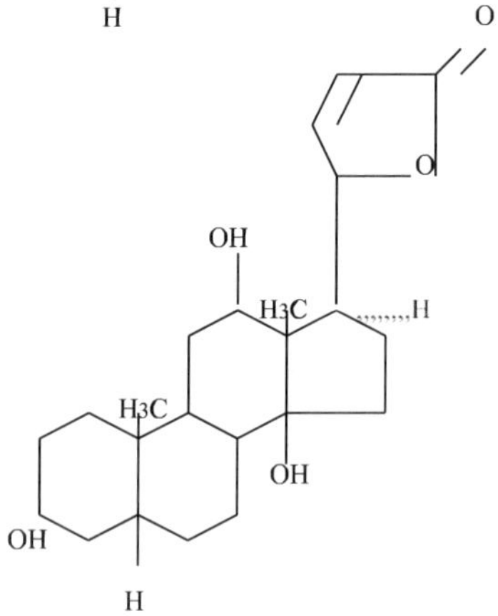

Digoxigenin

The glycone of digitoxin is composed of three digitoxe residues.

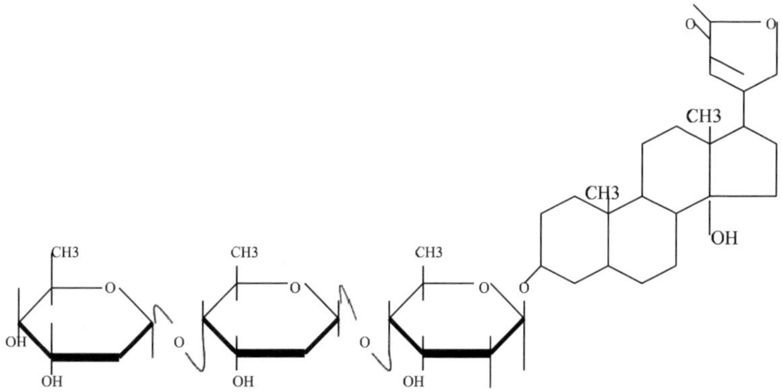

TANNINS

Tannins are one of a group of complex non uni form plant constituents consisting of bitter tasting polyphenols. The term tannins refers to the use of tannins in tanning hides into leather. However the term is widely applied to any large polyphenolic compound containing sufficient hydroxyls and other suitable groups such as carboxyls to form strong complexes with proteins and other macromolecules.

In the plant, tannins are defensive compounds that counteract bacteria and fungi by interfering with their surface proteins. They also deter herbivores by virtue of their astringent effect on the mouth and their interference with digestion. The 'tanning' of the proteins in the saliva and mucous membranes of the mouth cause the sensation of astringency; lubrication is reduced and the surface tissues actually contract.

Tannic acid

Occurs in many plants particularly in the bark of oaks and other members of the family *Fagaceae* and is used as a hemostatic agent, astrigent, and in the treatment of diarrhea. Gallic acid, the 3,4,5-Trihydroxybenzoic acid used for the same purpose is made from tannic acid or *nutgalls* (*oak apple; an excrescence on the oak*). Gallic acid is also found in gallnuts, sumac (*Rhus glabra, R. aromatica)* and tea leaves (*Camellia sinensis*) Tannins are classified in to two groups.

1. Hydrolysable tannins and

2. Condensed tannins.

Hydrolysable tannins are hydrolysed by weak acids or weak bases to produce carbohydrate and pheolic acid. At the center of hydrolysable tannin molecule there is a pylol carbohydrate. The hydroxyl groups of carbohydrate are partially or totally esterified with phenolic groups such as gallic acid (gallotannins) or ellagic acid (ellagitannins).

Condensed tannins are polymers of flavonoid units that are joined by carbon - carbon bonds, which are not susceptible to being cleaved by hydrolysis. While hydrolysable tannins and most condensed tannins are water soluble, some very large condensed tannin are insoluble.

Tannins extracted from the grapes are condensed tannins; hydrolysable tannins are extracted from the oak wood. Pomegranate fruit contain hydrolysable tannins. Most berries such strawberries, cranberries and blue berries contain both hydrolysable and condensed tannins.

Tannins may be medicinally used as antidiarroeal, hemostatic and antihemorrhoidal compounds. If ingested in excessive quantities, tannins inhibit absorption of minerals such as iron in to the body. This is because tannins are metal ion chelators and tannin-chelated metal ions are not bioavailable.

VOLATILEOILS

Volatile or ethereal oils are oils of the plant materials that are hydrophobic and contain volatile aromatic compounds from the plants. It is also called as the essential oil because it carries the distinctive scent of the plant. The most common essential oils are lavender, peppermint, eucalyptus, and clove oil.

Essential oils are usually extracted by distillation from the raw materials, consisting of the flowers, leaves, wood, bark, roots, seeds or fruit peels. The water condensed from the distillation process is referred to as *hydrosol, hydrolat, herbal distillate or plant water escence.* Egs. Rose water, lavender water.

Essential oils have medicinal properties that have been applied in folk medicine since ancient times and are still widely used today. Many have antiseptic properties. Aromatherapy is a form of alternative medicine, in which healing effects are ascribed to the aromatic compounds in essential oils and other plant extracts. They are used in perfumes and cosmetics, for flavouring food and drink, and for scenting incense and household cleaning products.

THE HOLISTIC APPROACH

Ayurveda is a holistic medicine. 'Holistic' is the adjective of 'holism', a Greek word *holos* meaning entire. Based on it, Ayurveda mainly concentrated to the belief of body, mind and spirit. Holistic approach is applicable to both the *rogi* (the patient) and *dravya* (the materials used for the treatment, including medicines and accessories).

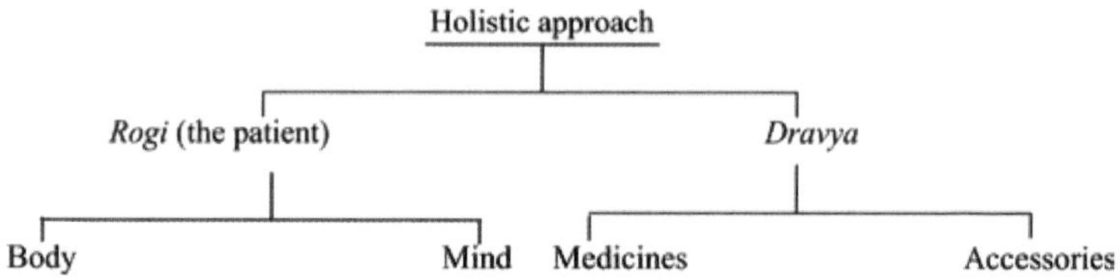

THE FUTURE OF AYURVEDA

As an alternative system Ayurveda has proven to be far more complex than our imagination could have conceived. But the therapeutic sustainability of Ayurveda is doubtful unless its pharmaceutical principles are scientifically explained. It is mostly commercialized as physical therapy and is developing in such an impressive display.

Treatment is the institution of measure or giving the remedies to cure disease. The explanation of c urative properties of a n administered drug should be unambiguously explicit and direct.

The basic structural units of all living organisms are cells, where thousands of chemical reactions take place. All organisms use the same molecules. The *Tridosha-Panchamahabhoota concept* was the 'struggle' to provide a coherent and accurate view of living process in a molecular basis when science was so primitive. Interpreting the life processes using such concepts and comparisons cannot bring up Ayurveda students to face the present complicated health issues. Ayurveda need not to be old always! It was contemporary at the time of its origin.

"A change" is the need of the hour, among the Ayurvedic students and practitioners. The five thousand year old concepts are still followed in the syllabus!

PLANT MEDICINES

The ancient Egyptians wrote the Ebers Papyrus, which contains information on over 850 plant medicines. Earlier Sanskrit writings such as the Rigveda and the Adharvaveda are some of the earliest available documents dealing with the medicinal knowledge that formed the basis of Ayurveda.

The abundant botanical resources of the tropical forests have already provided tangible medical advances, yet only one percent of the known plant and animal species have been thoroughly examined for the medicinal potentials.

'The discovery of digitalis in 1775 is accredited to the Scottish doctor William Withering, and makes for qui te an interesting historical story. While working as a physician in Staffordshire in the 18th Century, his girlfriend got him interested in plants and botany - so much so, that in 1776 he published a huge treatise, whose title begins '*A botanical arrangement of all the vegetables growing in Great Britain,...*' and goes on for a further 24 lines! By the age of 46 he had become the richest doctor outside of L ondon, and bought Edgbaston Hall in Birmingham, which is now Edgbaston Golf Club.

In 1775, one of his patients came to him with a very bad heart condition and since Withering had no effective treatment for him, thought he was going to die. The patient, being an independent type, went instead to a l ocal gypsy, took a secret herbal remedy - and promptly got much better!

When Withering heard about this, he became quite excited and searched for the gypsy throughout the by-ways of Shropshire. Eventually he found her, and demanded to know what was in the secret remedy. After much bargaining, the gypsy finally told her secret. The herbal remedy was made from a whole concoction of things, but the active ingredient was the purple foxglove, *digitalis purpurea.*

The potency of digitalis extract had been known since the dark ages, when it had been used as a poison for the mediaeval 'trial by ordeal', and also used as an external application to promote the healing of wounds. There are also reports of digitalis extract finding some use in the treatment of dropsy.

So, Withering tried out various formulations of digitalis plant extracts on 163 patients, and found that if he used the dried, powdered leaf, he got amazingly successful results. He introduced its use officially in 1785.

Even today, drugs based on digitalis extract, such as *Digitoxin* and *Digoxin*, are some of the best-known treatments to control the heart rate. It works by increasing the intensity of the heart muscle contractions but diminishing the rate, and doses as low as 0.3mg daily are all that is needed. Since *digitalis purpurea* contains a mixture of several cardiac glucosides and also several saponins in amounts and proportions, which vary with locality and with season, digitalis preparations vary considerably in potency and quality. Because of this, and the fact that the therapeutic dose is so small, it is very easy to exceed the safe dosage. Indeed, Withering recommended that the drug be diluted and administered repeatedly in small doses until a therapeutic effect became evident. This procedure was very effective in experienced hands, but was also very time-consuming. Nowadays, therefore, preparations from digitalis leaves are made using modern recrystallisation methods and are carefully standardised by bio-assay.

In 1799, Withering became very ill and it looked as though he was going to die. One of his friends, who was noted for his black sense of humour, commented '*The flower of Physic is withering...*' - a clever, if somewhat tasteless, pun. And when he finally died, his friends carved a bunch of foxgloves on his memorial.

INDEX

Page numbers followed by c, f and t refers to columns, figures and tables respectively.

E

F

L

M

N

T

U

V

W

X

Y

References.

Ch. Saa. 5.5, 8.3, 1.21

A.H Su 1/10

A.H. Sa. 347, 48

A.H. Su. 1.6

A.H. Su. 1.11, 1.8, 1.12, 1.14, 1.9, 10

A.S Ch 1 -7

Ch. Su. 8.4, 12.18, 8.7, 1.47, 1.54, 1.55

MN Chpt. Unmda Bhootonmada Nidana- 6 to 28

Phylosophy and terminology of Ayurveda, Prof. C.R. Agnivesh., Bsc. B.A.M, M.D (Ay)

Indian Philosophy: Chattopadhyaya. D (1986)

Indian Philosophy, Radhakrishnan, S (2006)

Biochemistry- Trudy McKnee, James R. McKee

Phytochemistry: Georges -Louis Friedli, Pg Dip., MSc., PhD.

Stedman's Medical directory

Indian Journal of Psychiatry, April 1987, 29 (2), pp. 127-123.

A complete guide to your emotions and your health –Emrika Padus

Other Titles In The Series

Adventure Of Consciousness

- *Yoga Chikitsa: Ashtanga Vinyasa Yoga/Giuliano Vecchiè*
- *Bhagwad Gita: Natyaroop in Hindi/ PK Agrawal*
- *Courage to Stand Alone: Conversation/ UG Krishnamurthy*
- *Dattatreya: The Way and the Goal/ Sri Jaya Chamarajendra Wadiyar Bahadur*
- *Mind is a Myth: Conversation/ UG Krishnamurthy*
- *Mystic of Enlightment: Conversation/ UG Krishnamurthy*
- *No way out: Conversation/ UG Krishnamurthy*
- *Presence of Siva/ Stella Kramrisch*
- *Thought is your enemy: Conversation/ UG Krishnamurthy*
- *Tirthankarasana: A Work On Jaina Yoga/ Shantilal D. Parakh. Dinesh S. Parakh*
- *Upanisads and Edith Stein: A Dialogue on Models of the Person/ Thomas Marottipparayil*
- *Yoga: Physiology, Psychosomatics Bioenergetics/ Andriy Safronov*
- *The Yoga Tradition: Its History, Literature, Philosophy and Practice/ Jorge Feuerstein*
- *Yoga-Patta: A Manual for Yoga Wall Practice/ Dmitry Danilov*
- *Yogatherapy/ Olena Akhramieieva*